ENGLISH RECUSANT LITERATURE
1558–1640

Selected and Edited by
D. M. ROGERS

Volume 129

JOHN COPINGER
A Mnemosynum
1606

JOHN COPINGER

A Mnemosynum
or Memoriall to the
Afflicted Catholickes
in Ireland
1606

The Scolar Press
1973

ISBN 0 85417 913 5

Published and Printed in Great Britain by
The Scolar Press Limited, 20 Main Street,
Menston, Yorkshire, England

1739503

A 10.5.68

MNEMOSYNVM
OR MEMORIALL TO
THE AFFLICTED
Catholickes in
Irelande.

*COMPREHENDED IN
2. bbockes. inthe one ther is a consolation for the sorovvfull, in the other a
resolution for the doubtfull. composed
by IOHN COPINGER priest,
bacheler of diuinitie, vvith an epistle
of S. Cyprian vvritten vnto the
Thibaritans, faythfullie translated by
the said authour.*

Printed.by Arnald du Brel!
of Tholosa, 1606.

ERRATA.

FOR,	READ.	PAGE
funne	funne	18
doth,	do	20
iues	ievves	21
intendeth	intende	29
hath	haue	32
taketh	take	32
pearels	pearles	32
eys	eyes	33
optained	obtained	34
mad	madê	35
contraire	contrarie	35
dolofull	dolefull	36
ecceleipse	eclypfe	36
mad	made	39
ich	itche	40
vr	or	40
coufound	confound	40
peruerth	peruerte	40
ther	their	41
ba	by	43
te	the	44
vvoes	vvoes	44

filde

ERRATA,

FOR	READ	PAGE
filde	feilde	45
moch	much	46
vvorketh	vvrought	46
suffer	suffered	47
tribulation	tribulations	48
neales	nailes	48
nealed	nailed.	48
saiih	faith	48
gotton	gotten	68
Ivvel	ievvel	69
stoot	stoute	69
be	he	77
forcc	force	79
reuatis	renatis	156
paltem	partem	156
sacerdoti	sacerdotem	242

F I N.

TO THE *VERTVOVS*,
and religious priestes , as also
the goodlie constant , and Ca-
tholick laitie of Ireland I. C.
vvisheth the grace of perse-
uerance in Chriest his catho:
church.

I Being *(louing bre-*
thrē and cuntrimē)
to performe a cer-
taine pilgrimage,
did heare there vvas a persecutiō
intended in our cuntrie againſt

ẽ

our catholick religion`, as also a
proclamation published against
the priestes & professors therof. I
thought good to defer my pur-
posed iourney to those holie reli-
kes, and to recollecte my self in
some place, that I may aswell de
clare my duetie to the catholick
church, in these her troubles &
persecutions, as also signifie vnto you my vnfained affectiõ, &
christian charitie in these your
aduersities. and seeing it is a diuine precept to loue our negbou-
res, and being affirmatiue, it bin-
deth vs to put it in execution in

their deſtreſſes and in time of neceſsitie. I thought good to comfort you in your ſorrovves, and to counſell you in your doubtes vvhich be vvorkes of mercie, & alſo to bevvayle your miſeries ſo the apoſtle did, vvhen he ſaid 2.Cor.11. quis infirmatur & ego non infirmor vvho is ſick or indiſpoſed, and I feele it not? So alſo did Iob vvhen he ſaid flebam ſuper eum Iob 30. qui afflictus erat & compatiebatur anima mea pauperi the: affliction of my negbour did cauſe me to vveepe, and his poouertie moued me to compaſsiö. I ſend ther-

fore *vnto you* this *Mnemosynum*
or memoriall *aswell for your*
consolation in your troubles, as
also for your resolution in your
doubtes, I made it first in Latine
and thought onlie to dedicat it
vnto the priestes and religious
of our nation, but being readie to
go to the presse, I *vvas perswa-*
ded by certaine graue religious
persons to translate it *vnto En-*
glish, being a language more *vul*
gare and comon vnto you, hoping
it may *vvork* some good effect in
such as could not vnderstand it
in the latine. and although my

onlie purpose is to spare no paines
vvhere I may do the greatest good
& dum tempus habemus bonum
operari to bestovv the residue of
my fraile life, and vncertaine
daies vvher e J may do god &
his church the best seruice,
yet I found great difficultie to ha
ue it printed in English for too
causes, the one, vvas, vvhat I
had to disraise my charges; I
should bestovvit in the printing
being a language altogether vn
knovven vnto the printer, and
therfore more charges and longer
time should be required, the other

ē   5

that I should be vvray my ovvne insufficiencie therin, vvhich vnto me is not so natural asvvell for my birth, as for my bringing vp. but I hope a fault in the language is not an offence before god, vvhich respecteth more the invvard intention of my hearte, then the out vvard characters by vvhich J declare the same. J desire you let not the improprietreof the English therof, nor the faultes, that did escape the printer vvhich vvas altogether ignorant of the same, giue occasion of loathsonesse of the matter, vvhich I hü-

blie craue at your handes to receaue vvith that deuotion and
intrals of charitie, by vvhich I
offer it : and for my labour and
charges bestovved therin, I beseech you as many as shall peruse
it, to saye one Aue Maria, that you
and I may die in the arcke vvith
Noe, that vvee may be saued in
the mountaine vvith Lott, that
vvee may liue and continue in
the catholick church and perseuere in gods fauour vntill the
last moment of our liues, vvhich
I beseech svveet Iesu to grant vnto you and me Amen; so fare vvell

ĕ   **4**

from the porte of S. Ma-
rie the laſt of Aprill
1606.

Your humble ſeruant

IOHN COP.

AFFLICTIONS, AND
troubles, are nothinge els:
then messengers: or pursewäts,
to call, and summon vs to god
vuhen vvee forsake him.

CAP. I.

IN all common mi-
series, and gene-
rall afflictions (lo-
uing bretheren,
and cuntrymen)
vve are bounde by the lavve

A

of god, and nature to bevvayle
our sinnes, for vvhich, vvee suffer
those miseries. to amēd, & reforme our liues, and to returne, and
conuert our selues vnto god,
vvhose haroldes, and messengers
troubles, and calamities be.

2. Para. 8.
20   So the good Kinge Iosaphat,
being oppressed vvith sundrie
troubles, & aduersities did returne vnto god (saieng) in our miseries, and calamites, this is the onlie remedie vve haue : that vvee
should lift vpp our eyes vnto
thee (ô god).

Ioel. 2   In the commune afflictions of
the people of Israell, the priestes
vvere commanded to prostrate
them selues, *inter vestibulum*, *&*
altare : betvrixt the entrie of the

temple, and the altar: at the feete
of god, and to crie out: lord saue,
and spare thy people, giue not,
thy inheritance, vnto the cruell
nations, to be of them troden vn
der foote, and despised.

The people also vvere commanded in fasting, mourning, la-
menting, and prayeng, to ren-
de ther hearts, and not there
garments. Thus Moyses, and *Num. 16
20. Exo-*
Aaron appeased gods vvrath a- *31.*
gainst that people : so did Dauid
in the mortalitie of his people,
flie vnto god, vvith contrition for
his sinnes, and purpose of améde- *2.1 Rege
ment : and the plague did cease: 24. 22. &
vit.*
the Niniuites did the like : so did *Iona 3 5*
Ezechias being sentensed to die, *Isa 33*
tourned his face against the vvall

A 2

and vvept: his sentence vvas re-
called:& Ezechias vvas repriued:
by giuing him 15. years to reforme his life. vvher vpon *S. Ambro*
se sayth. si noueris mutare delicta tua
Deus nouerit mutare sententiam
suam: if thou Knovveſt to change
thy vvicked life : god vvill alſo
change and alter his ſentéce paſt
againſt thee. Let vs follovv the
prophet ſaieng *derelinquat impius*
viam suam & vir iniquus cogita-
tiones suas,&c. Iſa.5 5. let the vvicked forſake his vvayes , and the
vngodly his vvicked thoughtes,
& let him turne vnto god becauſe, he is more inclined to pardon
vs, accordinge to his mercye: thé-
to punish according to his iuſtice.
In all theſe generall, and dolefull

Iſa. 35.

Amb sup.
Hom. in
Euang.

Iſa 55.

calamities , of our poore cuntrie:
so great as neuer any nation, vvas
subiect vnto: through vvarre , fa-
mine, plague, out of vvhich none
of that poore natiõ, escaped vvithout his portiõ, vvherein milliõs
did perish , & such as are liuing,
or did escape the svvorde : or the
miserable death of their neighbou
res, are oppressed: or rather ouervvhelmed : vvith such miseries:
& suche displeasant accidetes: as
it vvere better for them to end
ther miseries by death , then to
liue in continuall tormentes.

I vvill take no knovveledge, or
notice of suche as are the procu-
rers of your troubles. I vvould
vvhere the fault is committed, it
had rather bene reformed by the

A 3

then reproued by any other.

But surely the cause of such miseries, and afflictions, ought ra ther to be ascribed vnto our ovv ne grieuous offences , vvhich deserued greater plagues, and punishmentes:(if possiblye grea- ter could be inflicted), then vnto any other; for the authours are but god almighties instrumētes: to beate vs vvith his vvhipp ei- ther for the manifold sinnes, that vve haue cōmitted:that by the sa me vve may amend our liues: &be reduced vnto the filiale sub- iection,of our eternall father: or els:for the triall of our patience and curbinge vs, from fallinge into greater inconuenience like as the cunninge phisition:to preuent ſickneſſe to come, letteth the patiét blood in the ſpring time, taking from him, ſuperfluitie of blood, vvhich vvould ingender diſeaſes in the ſommer, not that the patient is ſicke, but leaſt he ſhoulde be ſicke.

Yf our miſeries be the debt, that are due, vnto the manifold treſpaſſes, that vve haue perpetrated: or the paine that ſhould follovv the outragious ſinnes, that vve haue cōmitted, vve ought to beare them patientlie, to embraſe them vvillingly, & to ſuffer the quietly.

It is vvritten in the booke of Iudith, that the capitaine of the children of Amon, called Achior, ſpeaking vnto Holophernes of the Ievves, is ſaied to haue ſpoke

lib. Iudith.c. 5.

A 4

after this forte : their god hateth
iniquitie,and vvickedneſſe, & ſo
our god hateth in vs catholickes vngolidneſſe : more then in
Ievves,pagans and heretickes. &
therfore no marueyle : being rebellious children vnto god : vve
should be punished like rebelles
and traiturs. it is notexpedient.
if vve offend god (as vvee haue
done) that vvee should hope for
a revvarde,vvhen vye haue deſer-
ued paine. If Achior the pagan
ſpake theſe vvordes ⸗ of the
Ievves . much more , a chriſtian
ought to ſpeake them of chriſtiãs.
if theſe afflictions be ſent vnto
vs,for our triall, and exerciſe of
uertue, vve ought not to grudge
at them : but rather to entertaine

them most gladly : & to say vvith the prophet. *proba me Deus* : & *scito cor meum* : & *cognosce semi-* *tas meas* : & *vide si via iniquitatis* *Psal. 136* *in me est,* & *deduc me in via eter-* *na psal.* 136. proue me ô god: sear- che my hearte : and discerne my steps : and see by the straihgt vvay vvhether I vvalke in the vvay of iniquite : and lead me by the vvay of euerlasting life.

Vvhereas novv our troubles rather increase , then decrea- se , by the last proclamation, vvhich vvas published in all pla- ces of Irelande: the last October. I can giue you no other reme- die: or comforte, then, *per patien-* *Cō.12.Ha* *tiam currere ad propositum nobis* *certamen ,* *aspicientes auctorem*

A 5

hebr. 14. *fidei consummatorem Iesum : qui*
proposito sibi gaudio , confusione
contempta crucem subijt , eum re-
cogitate , qui talem sustinuit aduer-
sus semetipsum contradictionem:
to runne, & go forvvard vnto the
battaile prepared for vs,and vvith
patience abide the brunt thereof.
let vs sayeth the apostle beholde
the authour of our fayth , vvhose onely ioye,vvas to beare,&en-
tertaine his crosse, and not respe-
cting the confusion, vnto vvhich
he vvas brought,neuer left of vntil he said *consummatum est*, it is a-
complished.remēber (saieth he)
that did suffer such reproches at
the handes of sinners.

Vnto you he drancke the bit
ter cup of his passion , vvhich

Chrieſt vvoulde haue to paſſe
vnto his church: and the members thereof.

For Chriſt being in the gar-
den of Gethſemani, in the darke
alone, flat vpon his face, ſvvea-
ting and praieng, and hauing
apprehended, the ſore agonie of
his bitter, and paynfull paſſion to
come, did not deſire of his father
eternall, that the elect of his
church should be cheriſed, vvith
poſſeſſiõs, or vvorldly pampered:
but of that cup he vvould giue
them a draught to drincke.

This holy cup of Chrieſt:
is no other thing, but tẽptation,
hunger, colde, thirſt, perſecutiõs,
exile, pouertie, and martyrdome
of vvhich thinges god giueth to

drinck, and to taſt, to ſuch, as he
hath choſen, to ſerue him, and
hath predeſtinated, to be ſaued.

A ſtomacke that is ful of bad
and corrupte humours: and a body, that languiſheth through diſ-
feaſes, muſt take a ſovver purga-
tion: vvherby, the one ſhoulde be
clenſed of the humoures: and the
other healed of the ſickneſſe.
Shall not a miſerable ſoule, infected, vvith the poyſon of ſinne, &
corrupted vvith ſundrie vices, take this holſome potion, and pur-
gatió of Chrieſt his cup? vvherby, it ſhould be clenſed, of the
diſeaſe : and lighted of the
heauie burden, of malignant
humoures. Shall not a putrified
vvounde, be healed, by a hoat iró?

shall not vvee therefore, that are
catholickes, and chriſtiãs onely in
name, but contrarie vnto Chriſt
in our vvourkes: and perſecutors
of Chriſt, and his church: in our
purpoſes ſo incõſtãt, ſo malicious
in our vvilles, ſo hypocriticall: only bearing a shevve of fained ho-
lines before man, but before god,
vvho is the ſearcher of our heartes, are ſoũd ſtubble, & dry ſprig-
ges fit for hell fire, shall not vvee
(I ſay,) be purified by the fire of
tribulatiõ? & be chaſtiſed by the
rodd of affliction? to the end, vve
might be made perfecte mẽbers,
of Chrieſt his church: tryed and
vvell trayned ſouldiers in the cã-
pe of Ieſus.

But I feare very much, that the

grieuouse, and lamentable complaint of Ezechiel, is meant of vs
Ezec. 4.33 by *fili hominis*, &c. I haue put the
house of Israel (saith he) into a for
nace of the captiuitie of Babylon
hoping, that being within the
fire of tribulation, she would resolue to pure gold, and fine siluer:
but she is conuerted into leather,
lead, brasse, and Iron.

This is the meaning of the
holy ghost in this text, that man
is conuerted into lead, who
being put into the fornace of tribulation, cannot only not be
amended, but from one day to
another grouve worse, and worse: that man becomes yron, to
whom god hauing sent some
punishment, to aduertise him,

in place to be amended, he cea-
seth not to repine at it. He is turned into leather, vvho outvvar-
dly seemes to be of holie lyfe, &
vvhen any tribulatiõ happeneth,
he is foũd an hypocrite, aud that
man is resolued into brasse, vvho
in his dispositiõ, is intractable, in
his condition inflexible, in his life
carelesse, & in his cõsciẽce negli-
gẽt: so as I feare much that there
are farre greater nũber of such as
by tribulatiõs, are conuerted into
yron, leather, brasse: and lead, thẽ
of them vvhich become gold or
siluer. god deliuer you in al your
troubles from the like transmu-
tation, and giue you the grace to
make better profite of your tribulations.

Assuring our selues that they be the only vvayes vnto the King dome of heauen, For by them the blessed sainctes did enter into glo-rie: aud hauing passed ouer the tempestuous vvaues of this mise-rable vvorld, novv they cry out and say *transiuimus per ignem, & aquam: & eduxisti nos in refrige-rium:* vvee passed through fire and vvater: and at length thou hast brought vs vnto our expe-cted end and desired rest.

Psal 65.

Vnto these Christ did drin-cke his cup: vvhich is the signe of those that shall be saued. he said vnto the sones of zebedei: *potestis bibere calicem?* &c. can ye drinke of the cup, of vvhich I must drincke? 3. Math. 20. of this cup

Ma.3.no.

D auid

Dauid fard : *calicem falutaris acci-*
piam Pf. 115. I vvill. accept and T/. 115.
receue at the handes of my fa -
uioure the hoalfom cup of affliction: and then vvill I call vppon
his name.

For vve cannot efcape hell,
butt at the coft of great trauaile.
The fvvoard of fainct Peter : the
croffe of fainct Andrevve : the
knief of fainct Bartholome : the
gratyron of fainct Laurence : and
the sheares of fainct Steuen : the
fvvoard of grief of the bleffed virgine: the generall calamities of all
the fanctes : vvhat other thinges
are they, but certaine badges they
haue receaued of Chrieft: and cer-
tame gulpes they haue fvvallo
vved of this cup: and certaine

B

lances vvher vvith they vvere let
blood. leaſt the ſuperfluitie therof
in the heate of the ſunne should
corrupt the ſoule.

So many degrees, vve ſhal receaue in   heauen, of glorie : as vve
haue drūcke of the cup of Chrieſt
in this life. the prophet ſayth *ſe-*
Pſal. 92. *cundum   multitudinem   dolorum*
meorum : in corde meo conſola-
tiones tuæ lætificauerunt animam
meam: accordinge to the meaſure,
and quantitie of the ſorovves, and
afflictions of oure penſiue contri-
te hearte, in this vvorld: oure ſoule
shalbe comforted, and made ioyfull in the celeſtiall paradice. and
therefore vve ought to pray vnto
god. euerieday, vvith teares, that, if
vvee cannot drincke all his eupe,

at the leaſt: that he vvould ſuffer
vs to taſt thereof. the cupp of
Chrieſt: althoughe it be bitter in
drinckinge: after the drinckinge
therof, it doth great profitt. I
vvould ſay the troubles vvhich
vve ſuffer, to be good, they giue
not ſo muche paine, vvhenvve indure them: as they after vvardes,
giue pleaſure, hauinge paſſed
them, let Dauid fanſie the cold
vvater of Bethelem, let the glutton in hel cry out vnto Abraham
for the leaſt drope of any licour,
or any moiſture, let the couetuous gape after riches or the
drounckard thirſt aftervvine: but
for the conſolation and ſaluation
of a chrieſtan: ther is nothinge ſo
neceſſarie for him then that he

should drincke of this cup.

Ther is another cup, vvhich is
called the cup of the vvrathe of
god:vvherof, to speake the intra-
les:doth open, the members doth
quacke,the hearte doth faile, the
fleash doth tremble: the guiltie
conscience doth torment, the eys
doth vveepe, and oure imagina-
tion doth vex vs vvith the appre-
hension thereof. vvith this cupe
god doth threaten vs. This is that,

Iſ.ſi. vvhich the prophet speaketh of:
va tibi Hierusalim quia bibiſti ca-
licem iræ Dei vſque ad fæces, vvo
be vnto thee Hierusalim, be cause thoue haſt sucked, the cup of
oure lordes vvrath euen vvto the
dregges,he drincketh, the cup of
vvrath,that falleth frõ the ſtate of

graee, vvherin heftoód. vvhereof
it follovveth, that the foule is muche more dead, vvithout grace:
then a bodie vvithout a foule. of
this cup the vnfortunat Synagoge did make hir felf druncke : and
the druncknesse of this , vvas the
caufe, that Ifrael vvas banished:
from Iudea : and tranflated vnto
Babylon : and alfo that of godes
inheritáce: and his vineyarde thofe Iues vveare depriued : vvhich
vvas giuen vnto the gentiles : and
this vvas the caufe, that the catholick religió:and godes taberna
cle, vvas taken from many chriftian countrys: and did pafle ouer
vnto the eaft , and vveaft indies.
and novve fuch as vveare good
chriftians in time paft, are becom

C 3

infidels and subiect vnto Turckes,
pagans, mahometistes, and heretickes: and in steed of the catholicke religion they do embrace the
rites of paganisme Mahometis-
me, Iudaysme: and Caluinisme.
and trulie, it is godes iust punishment: seinge, they did not obey
the true pastore, that they
should be confounded by false
prophetes: and for that they haue
forsaken the catholicke religion of
Chrieft they should be peruersly
mislead and intoxicated vvith ma
ny false religions. this vvas pro-
phesied of this people in the
scripture. thiefe be they that did
drincke the groundes and dregges
therof, vntil nothinge vvas left:
thiefe vveare they that made a

Matb. 24.
9. Iob. 5.
43. 1. Ti
moth. 4. 1.
2. Tim. 3 1.
2. pt. 3.

shipvvreacke of ther fayth by for-
fakinge ther ancient religion, by
denieinge all the articles of chri-
ftianiti e: thiefe be they, of vvhom
the p rophet complayneth *excuf-* | Hier. c. 2.
ferunt iugum Domini, & diripue-
runt vincula eius, they haue caft
of the yocke of oure lorde, they
haue brocken his giues and fetters: thiefe be they of vvhom the
forefayd prophet fpeacketh *dereli-*
querunt me fontem aquæ viuæ, &c.
they haue forfaken me beinge the
fontaine of life, and haue made
vnto them filues cifternes that
cannot containe any vvater, thiefe be they, that haue drounʒē the
cup of euerlaftinge vvoo, by
vvhofe miferable forfaxinge of
the catholicke fayth, by vvhofe

B 4

manifeſt contempt and deſpiſinge
of all ſacrifices, ſacramentes, rites,
and religious ceremonies, thovv-
ſandes haue bene miſerablie per-
uerted, and millions left in endles
vvoe.

I hope this is not the cup that
you drincke of, but the cup of
the paſſiõ of Chrieſt, not the cup
of the Synagoge, but the cup
that oure ſauioure in the gardẽ did
drinck of, by vvhich he vvould
haue his churche to be cheriſhed.
of the one vvhoſoeuer drincketh
he doth ſvvallovv hel, of theo-
ther heauen. the one hath a ſvveet
taſt indrinckinge but aftervvades,
a terrible ſmarte, the other ſovver
in drinckinge, but after vvardes,
giueth health, vnto him, that
drin

drincketh therof. *nulla remedia tam faciunt dolorem quam ea quæ funt falutaria* : ther is no remedie fo hoaffom as fuch that caufeth the greateft fmarte.

Cice. ad quint. frat.

This cup of tribulation , yvas fo bitter, as none could drincк the fame, vntil Chrieft, did beginn it vnto vs, in the apprehenfion of his paffion, and in the anguishe of his extreame paine.

None could drincke the vvaters of mara vntil Moyfes did caft his rod, into it, and beinge bitter before, vvas after vvardes made fvveet and pleafant. the croffe of Chrieft, and all other tribulations, vveare infamous, and diffonerable vnto thofe, that beare and fuffred them. but novve by

Exod. 15. *nuмe.* 33.

B 5

the death of Chrieſt, the croſſe is renovvmed in the vvorld , and tribulariõs,ſuffred for his ſake,are more ſvveet,then the honie cõbe. and this bleſſed croſſe beinge caſt into the vvaters of afflictions, *ſons*

Io. 4.   *aquæ ſalientis in Ʋiiam æternam a fontaine* of vvater runninge vnto life euerlaſtinge , ſprmgeth out of them.

Thieſe be the afflictions , that chriſtians ought alvvayſe,to deſi- re of god , thieſe be the tribula- tious,that vertuous people ought to embrace, as ſent from god, and thieſe by the fatherlie corrections, by vvhich vve ought to returne vnto god if vve haue forſaken him.

The godlie people that vvent
be

be fore did aſſure vs , and vve by
daylie croſſes of the good and the
proſperitie of the vngodlie ought
to beleue the ſame, that ther is no
greater temptation , then not to
be tempted, no greater trouble
then not to be troubled , no grea-
tet chaſtiſment , then not to be
chaſtiſed, nor no greater vvhip,
then not to be ſcurged of god. let
vs therfore follovve the counſell
of the apoſtle *exhibeamus nos*   2. *Cor. 6.*
metipſos in multa patientia, in tri-
bulationibus, &c. Let vs(ſayth he)
as the ſeruantes of god behaue
oure ſelues in much patiéce, abide
muche troubles , ſuffer tribula-
tious, diſtreſſes, paines, anguishes,
perplexities, laboures and paine,
let vs ſaith he yeeld oure ſelues
vnto

vnto the auftere vvorkes of
pennance,of long vvatchinge,mu-
che faftingeand all other religious
exercifes. Let vs shevve oure felues in chaftitie and vnfayned charitie,mortified,but alvvaife liuing
chaftifinge of our felues, but not
dead therby, becaufe this is the
time,that iudgment,should begin

1.Te.1.4. at the hovvfe of god-as fancte Peter fayth.and as the prophet fpeaketh *cum accepero tempus*, &c.
Vvhen I shall haue leafure I vvill
examine, and iudge thy righteouf

Pf.74.
Iob. 9. nes of vvhich time Iob fayth. *Ve-*
rebar omnia opera mea, &c. I did
feare all my vvorkes , kuovvinge
that god fpareth not to punishe
a finner-againft vvhome the finne is committed. do not therfore
                              feare

feare them, that killeth the bodie.
but feare him rather, that can caft
both foule, and bodie vnto the
pit of hell. our fauiour faith. all
that confeffeth me, before man. *Maih. 10.*
him vvill i confes before my father, vvhich is in heauen. *tradent*
enim vos in tribulationem, &c. they *Maih 5*
vvil fayth he, procure youre trou-
ble. augment your torment: caufe *maih.25.*
you to beflaine. many falfe prophetes fhall rife and fhall feduce
many. iniquitie. fhall aboude. charitie fhall vvax colde. vvho fœuer
fhal continue, vnto the end fhalbe faued. for this ende vve ftriue.
euen vnto death againft all the
princes of darcknes: and againft all
thofe that intendeth to debare
and hinder vs therof.

And

And becaufe that god is the end
of oure peregrination: the centre
of oure mouinge, the confolation
of oure troubled mindes : the
Knovvledge of oure vnderftan-
dinge, the obiect of ourë loue, the
defire of oure heartes : the quiet-
neffe.and reft of oure languished
fpirit:the felicitie thatvvee longe
for,and the ioy thatvvee hope for:
vvho vvill not fuffer vs,to taxe reft
or conforte in any earthly thinge
but in him felf,let vs therfore follovve him.euen as the iuie taketh
no reft,vppon the earth, vntill, it
getteth fom tree; or vvall , by
vvhich it may be lifted vpp: fo
oure poore foule taketh no reft in
any earthlie thinge:eyther gold:
or filuer vntill it cõ vnto god. and
find

finde him.and therfore sainct Augustin had reason to say *Dominé fecisti me propter te & cor meum non quiescit quousque venerit ad te:* thoue haste made me o lorde for thy self, and my soule, shall neuer be at rest, vntill it shall com and arriue vvith thy self, in the place of youre felicitie. vvith reason the said authoure saith: *non est quies* ^lib. 4. conf. *vbi illam quæritis. quærite quod quæritis, sed non est vbi quæritis, quæritis beatam vitam in regione mortis? non inuenietis. quomodo vitam inuenietis vbi viuere pœna est ?* there is no rest vvhere you secke it : you may searche it but you shall not finde it.do you aske a happie liefe in the region of death ? but you shall not find it. hovve canst thoue

find

find lief, vvheare there is nothinge
but death? vvhy shoulde vvee expect any ioy or felicitie in the
kingdom of paine, and miseries? if
Chrieft accordinge to his diuinitie, beinge the maker, and creator
of thevvorlde, had no place of rest
therin : vvhen he saith the foxes
hath ther hoales : the birdes alfo
there neaftes : but the fon of man
hath not a place to put in his head.
the birdes, that be in cages though
they be made of gold and precious
pearels, taketh no rest therin. moyfes tooke no pleasure in Pharaos
court, Iofeph not vvith ftãding all
the riches of ægipt tooké no rest
beinge in prison and vve that are
in the prison of this miferable car-
kafe thoughe it be loadẽ, and furnished

nished vvith neuer so much riches or vvealth can haue no rest
nor ioy therin. in the vvay ther is
no rest but in the end. vnto,
vvhich, the vvay leadeth, is rest.
in the centre of oure mouinge
is rest. and not in the motion it
self. it is a certaine infaillible
principle, amonge phylosophers
that nothinge hath rest, vntill it
cometh vnto his end. as the riuers, hath no rest, vntill they com
vnto the sea: neyther the stone vn
till it cometh vnto the cētre: neyther the fire, vntill it comethvnto
his ovvne sphere, much les the
soule of mā vntill it cometh vnto
god, vvhich cannot be found vppon the earth, vvhich cannot be
seene vvith corporal eys, ney ther

C

optained, or gottē by earthlie, and
corruptible defires. the trueth
vvherof is verified, vnto vs, by fāct
lib. 10. conf. Auguftin faynge : *exifti anima*
mea ad contemplanda ea quæ funt, per
quinque fenfus: dic mibi aliquid de deo
meo, nunquid inuenifti illum; &c? O
my foule, haue you fent forth
youre corporall fiue fenfes, to be
holde the earthe ? I pray tell me
fom thinge, of my god : haue you
found him, vppon the earthe ? *dic*
mihi vbi pafcat? vbi cubet in meridie?
ne vagari incipiam quærens eum: the
fpoufe demandeth in the canticles: vvhere doth he lodge, leaft
I fhoulde go aftray, feekinge him
in the vvorlde : vvher vve may
not finde him, much les enioy
him: the foule anfvvered and faid I

fought him vppon the, earth and, I could not find him. I fought for him of all other thinges, and they told me that vvhat I fought vvas not in them, and that they could yeld vnto me no reft: if I fought the fame in them. and they them felues vveare ordained, and mad, to com vnto him, in vvhom I should haue reft. therfore deere brethren, and contrimen do not expect peace nor quietneffe in a vvorld of difcord: and troubles: do not loocke for tranquilitie in boiftrous feas: ful of dangerons vvaues· and contineuall fearfull tempeftes: do not hope to liue for euer in à bodie fo corruptible as this, vvhich is cōpofed of corruptible, and contraire qualities,

vvhich of force must bedissolued:
do not gape for felicitie in a lief
so shorte:so vncertaine: so muta-
ble.so deceit ful:so miserable:and
so subiect to dolofull lottes, and
doubfull endes. vvhere vve can
haue no rest:vvher euerie thinge
by the essential and naturall prin-
ciples of vvhich it is framed, and
compacted, is subiect to strange
alterrations, and mutationes:
vvher euerie one that hunteth
after the lamentable pleasures
therof,are sure to suffer eccleipse
euery moment, vvhere vve feele
so many displeasant accidentes
and dissastruous euentes, as ther
are instances in oure beinge,ther-
fore let vs say vvith the prophet
satiabor quando apparuerit glo-

Pf.16.

ria tua I shal neuer be fatisfied,
vntill I beholde and fee thy glorie in thy ovvne kingdomë,vvhe-
re you giue it abundantly, not in
this vvreatched vvorlde: vvher
euery thinge yeldeth but loath
somnesse. here vve must lament,
andvveepe:that vvee may reioice
ther. here vve must be sadd that
there vvee may be glad. *qui hic fe-* P.f.125
minãt in lachrimis ibi in exultatione
metent:vvhofoeuer fovveth heere
in teares shall reape there vvith
ioy.

C 3

THE TROVBLES,
by vvhich god vifited the
iuſt, are exercifes of there pa-
tience: occafions of there me-
rites, augmentations of godes
grace, and means to increafe
and expreffe his glorie in thẽ.

CHAP. II.

F god be more
pleafed, and glori-
fied, for the affli-
ctions, that vve do
indure and for
the trauailles that vve fuffer,
then for the delighres vvherin

vve vvallovve: and for the profperitie that vvee do enioy? vvee
ovght rather to aske of god patiéce,to beare,the one : then longe
lief,and quiet reft to poffeffe the
other.for as the prophet faith *ad-*
iutor eft in tribulationibus quæ in-   *Pſ. 45.*
uenerunt nos nimis the more vve
be oppreffed vvith tribulations,
the more he hath an eye tovvardes vs,and fo he faid in the 87.   *87.*
Pſal. *de quacunque tribulatione cla-*
mauerunt ad me exaudiam eos, &c.
in vvhat foeuer tribulation they
shall be , I vvill heere them. by
vvealth,and profperitie, vve forget god : beinge affrighted: vvith
feare,beingetroubledvvith grief,
vve turne,and flie vnto him : and
are mad more perfect and do re-

couer more ftrength againft oure
enymies *cum infirmor, tunc fortior
fum*:the apoftle faid, that vvhen
he vvas fick, then vvas he moft
ftronge:becaufe the fickman doth
neyther fvvel by pride, nor cōcu-
pifcence doth vex him:or auarice
doth ich, or inuie dorh inflame.
or ire doth alter:ur glutony doth,
coufound:or flouth fulneffe doth
make negligent, or ambi-
tion doth peruerth. and for that
*Pf.*114. caufe the holy prophet faith *tribulationem & dolorem inueni: & no-
men Domini inuocaui* beinge compaffed vvith tribulatiou, and affli-
ctiō, I fledvnto god for fuccoure
this is a fpecial means, by vvhich
god calleth vs vnto him felf, that
beinge fcourged in the vvorld,

vve should forfake it and fo turne: vnto god *imple facies eorum
ignominia & quærent te Domine:*
bringe thē vnto cofufiō,and they
vvill acknovvledge thy name.
Nabugchodonofor beinge tranf- *Daniel.* 4.
formedvnto a beaft:did perceaue
his offence and confeffed god. *Luc.*15.
the prodigall childe neuer returned home vntill by force of aduerfitie he vvas compelled. *in an-
gufltia requifierunt te Domine* in
tker anguishes they feeke thee. *Ifa.*26.
ther is a remedie for euery difea-
fe:a cure for euery foare , a falue
for euery fikneffe.fo afflictions be
the only medicionable drugges:
and medicines that do heale,
and cure the dieafe of finne , and
as the ficknes is great:fo the cure

and phisicke muſt be accordingly:
ſo oure troubles and miſeries to
haue a proportion vnto oure
vvickednes, vvhich vve haue co-
mitted: muſt be no les then oure
offences vvhervvith they ſhould
be cured. the phyſiciō alſo ought
tobe expert, and cūning vvhich is
god againſt vvhome the iniquitie
is committed. as ſainct Auguſtine
ſaith: intelligat *homo medicum eſſe*

Aug. ſu-
per Tſ. 21.

deum: & tribulationes eſſe medica-
mentum ad ſalutem : non pænam ad
damnationem: ſub medicamento poſi-
tus vreris, ſecaris, clamas , non audit
medicus ad voluntatem: ſed audit ad
ſanitatem: let manknovve ſaith he,
that god is a phyſicion , and that
tribulations are receiptes for oure ſaluation, and n ot puniſhemēt

for oure damnation : and being
vnder cure , the vvounde being
cutt, the vlcer being brente : god
heareth not at youre leasure, vntill the putrified soare be heale d:
vvhich cannott be don be prosperitie, and therfore aduersitie is
very expedient as the said authoure *said : nullus seruus Christi*
sine tribulatione est: si putas te non
habere persecutiones: non dum cæpisti
esse chrsstianus : ther is no seruant
of Chriest vvithout tribulation:
if thoue doest not purpose vvith
thy self to suffer persecutions
thoue art not a christian. do not
feare to be afflicted . but to be
disinherited. vnto vvhich agreeth
sainct Gregorie: *aurem cordis tri-*
bulatio aperit: quam sæpe prosperitas

Aug. in quadā ho.

Greg.in
hoau sup.
Euang.

huius mundi claudit.si iniquus quis-
que in hac vita permittitur prospe-
rari necesse est, vt electus Dei debeat,
sub fiagello frœni retineri : vve be
said he insensible vnto godes in-
spirations, throgh prosperitie. and
by aduersitie vvee heare vvhat
he vvill haue vs to do. if this
be te only place, vvheare the
vvicked haue ther solace : it
must be the onlie place vvhere the good: and godlie must be
subiect to voes and miseries, by
vvhich he may be keipt and re-
strayned frō the iniquitie of sinn,
as by the bridle of correction.

Abraham said vnto the ri-
che vvorldly glutton thoue
art novve tormented vvith paine , thoue hast receaued thy

paye in the vvorlde and hafte re-
pofed thy felicitie in the pleafa-
res therof, and faid Lazarus to be
in reft, becaufe he liued in miferies, vvhē he vvas in this trafitorie
life, vvhich fainct Bernard confi-
dereth fainge:

Sumus in hoc mundo quafi in   *D. Ber.*
campo certaminis , &c. vve are
faith he in this vvorld , as in the
filde , vvhere the battle is
giuen, and vvho foeuer abideth
no hardneffe , plagues , and tribulations, he muft departe hince
inglorious.

Neyther let this difmaye you,   *D.Greg. in*
that god in this vvorlde thus *quadam ho*
chaftifeth the good. vvhen he
knovveth, vvhat is beft for them
vvhich S.Gregorie noteth fainge

cum recognosco Iob in sterquilinio:
Ioānem esurieniem in eremo: Petrum
extensum in patibulo : Iacobum de-
collatum ab Herodis gladio : cogito
qualiter Deus cruciabit,quos repro-
bat,qui ita dure affligit quos amat:
vvhen I beholde faith he Iob
vppon the dunghil replenished
vvith the deformitie of boches,
Iohn hungrie in the defarte , peter hauinge his head dovvn vvarde vppon the croffe, Iames be
headed by the fvvoard of Herod:
Ido meditate vvith my felf:hovve
vvill he tormente the reprobate,
feinge he doth fo feuerlie puuishe
them:vvhome he loueth.

Thiefe godlie people vveare
not fomoch glorified , by the miracles that they vvoarketh : as by

the tribulations, that they suffer. euen as ftares, vvhich in the
daye time cannot be feene, in the
night they shine , fo treue vertue vvhich in profperitie cannot
be difcerned, doth shevv it felf in
aduerfitie.

Dauid (as caffiodorus faith) in
his greateft tribulations.did com
pofe the fvvceteft pfalmes.vvher-   *Pfal.89.*
fore he faid *lætati fumus pro diebus
quibus nos humiliafti: annis quibus
vidimus mala:* bleffed be the days
in vvhich thoue haft vifited vs
vvith thy corrections.the bleffed
fainctes did defire of god this vi-
fitation, fainct Auguftine did ear-   *S. Aug.*
niftlie defire of god not to be for
gotten herin fainge:*hic vre, hic,
feca, vt in æternum parcas.* burne

and cut me a fundre, here that
thoue maist spare me for euer.
vnto thiese blessed sainctes nothinge is more svveet then the tribulation of this life, becaufe in
fuffrioge them patientlie they
imitate Chrieft his patience, and
remember Chrieft his paffion.
the churche fingeth:o svveet nea-
les, vvith vvhich oure fauioure
vvas nealed, by reafon of the
svveetneffe of his bleffed paffion,
vvhy should not oure teares
beinge shed for him, be svvet vn-

D. *Bern.*

to vs.S.Bernard faiih *delitiæ ange-*
*lorum funt lachrimæ veftræ:*the ioys
and delightes of the angels are
oure vvepinge.and in his boock
of the contempt of the vvorld,
he faid *felices* lachrimæ *quas beni-*
gnæ

*gnæ manus conditoris abstergunt. & beati oculi, qui in talibus liquefieri potius elegerint·quam eleuari in superbiam:quam omne sublime videre: quam auaritiæ, & petulantiæ famulari:*blessed be the teares, vvhich the bountifull, and milde handes of oure sauioure clensed, and vviped avvay:and blessed be the eys, that are rather dissolued vnto mourninge, and vveepinge : then proudly lifted vpp on high : or abused in the vvourkes of vngodlinesse.

Blessed vvere the teares of the prophet vvhen he said: *lachrimis meis stratum meum rigabo* Ps. 6. I *Ps.6.* did vvash my bed vvith teares, and blessed be the teares of mary Magdalin by vvhich she vvashed *Luc 7.*

D

her soule from the filth of
sinn. and blessed be the teares , of the sainctes , vvhich
Christ clenseth and vvipeth a

Apoc.y.21 vvay.

If ther be a vvoe pronunced
against laughinge : vvoe be vnto
Luc. 6. youe (saith Christ), that laug-
heth : for youe shall bevvayle
and vveepe. so saith Salomon
Par.Sal.14 *risus: dolore miscetur : & extre-*
ma gaudii luctus occupat. hinc
iterum dixit risum reputani erro-
rem : & gaudeo, dixi, quid fru-
Eccl.2. *stra deciperis.*   Laughinge (said
he) shalbe mingled vvith
Prouer.10. griefe : and much gladnesse in
14. this vvorlde, is subiect to much
affliction. and therfore he saith
I haue esteemed laughinge to

be mœere follie. I faid vnto
all paftimes, and playe vvhy
are you deceaued. and fo
he faith, *cor fapientum ʋbi* ᴱᶜ
*triſtitia eſt: cor ſtultorum ʋbi
lætitia*: the heart of the vvife
is pofeffed vvith fadneffe: but
the hearte of the foole is becom vvanton and diffolute for
ioy and mirth.

Vvhy should not vve de-
plore oure finnes, and vvith
vvepinge eys vvashe them a
vvay: and blott them out of
godes memorie, that oure na-
mes may be recorded in the
bœocke of lief. vvhy should
nott vvee lament in thiefe
miferable dayes, that oure ta-
bernacle be taken from vs the

D 2

children of Iſrael did more lamente,that,they had not the vſe
of there religion, at Hieruſalim,
out of vvhich, they vveare bani-
ſhed: then for there captiuitie in
Aëgipt,by vvich they haue bene
depriued of ther libertie , and
made ſlaues vnto ther enimies.
they neuer ceaſed to crie *ſuper*

Pſ.136. *flumina Babylonis fleuimus dum*
recordaremur tui ſyon : by the ri-
uerſide of Babylõ vve do vveepe
and lamente,vvhen vve remember t hee O Syon. ſainge *quomodo*
cantabimus canticum Domini in
terra aliena: hovv can vvee ſinge
the ſonge of oure lorde, in a-
ſtrange lande. the like Dauid
hath don ſainge : *fuerunt mihi la-*

Pſal. 41. *chrimæ panes die ac noƐte dum dici-*

tur mihi quotidie vbi est Deus tuus:
I coulde not eate my breadvvith-
out teares, vvhen itvvas said vnto
me, vvhere is thy god. the blef-
sed MarieMagdalin did vveepe at *Mtt. 16.*
oure sauiours sepulchre, becaufe *2.Reg. 22.*
shee could not find him,the children of Ifrael did more lamente,
that the philiftins, had taken
from them the arcke of oure lorde,then for the victorie,that they
had lofte , or for the ovver-
throvve they fustained . the
three kinges of the eaft vveare
much greeued , vvhen they
loft the ftare, that should leade
them vnto Chrieft. vvhen the
blessed virgineloft oure fauioure,
she could neuer be at reft, vntill
shee found him , the prophet *Pfal.41.*
D 3

cried out and said *sitiuit anima mea ad deum fontem viuum, quando veniam & apparebo ante faciem Dei mei*: my soule thirsted after my god vvhich is the liuelye fontaine of the vvater of lief. and

Pl.42 in another place he said : *quemadmodum desiderat ceruus ad fontes aquarum , &c.* euen as the stagge desireth the springes of vvater euen so my soule longeth after thee o god. vvhat lamentatiō the

Hier. [6].[5]. prophet Hieremie made. *Recordare, Domine, quid acciderit nobis, &c.* remember o lord vvhat happned vnto vs: behold oure inheritaunce did passe ouer vnto strangers I meane oure religion shalbe taken from vs, and shalbe giuen vnto the gentiles, and oure selues shalbe depriued therof. vvhat a lamantable cafe it should be, if god vvould fuffer youe to be giuen, and deliuered vnto the licentious gofpell of Caluin: to be blinded vvith herefie, to be confounded vvith falfe prophetes, to be caft out of the arcke of Chrieft his church, to be pufte vpp vvith euerie blafte of erronuous doctrine and phantafticall opinious, to be cut of, and difmembred out of the catholicke church, vvhich youe haue obeyed from the beginninge, vntill theife miferable daies, and to be depriued of the merittes, of Chriefte his paffion, of vvhich none is partaker, butt,

D 4

such, as do hold them selues
vvithin his church. and to be se-
parated from god, from Chriest,
and from all his sanctes: of all miseries is the chiefest. and for
t hat cause the saidholie prophet
saieth *pone me Domine iuxta te, &*
cuiusuis manus pugnet contra me,
ioyne me o lorde vvith thy self
and I care not if all the
streinght of man be against me,
this is the onlye thinge, that Dauid sought of god so earniestlie
sayinge: *vnam petii a Domino. hanc*
requiram, vt inhabitem in domo Do-
mini omnibus diebus vitæ meæ: one
thinge I sought of god, and the
same all the dayes of me life I
vvill aske of him, that I may dvvell
in the house of oure lord all the

Hier.

Ps.26.

dayes of my life, and fo he faid
Vias tuas Domine demonſtra mihi,
&c. Shevve vnto me (o lord) thy
vvays and teache me thy ſteppes.

This is that vvhich Chrieſt
faith in the gofpell, that one
thinge vvas neceſſarie.

Such as be Zealous of godes
honore, and haue any care of ther
ovvne ſaluatiõ, should ſooner ſuffer all afflictions, then to make a
shipvvreacke of ther religion, to
ſuffer them ſelues, tobe ſeparated
from cuntry, from vvife, and children, from all the vvorld: rather
then to be ſeparated from the catholicke church, though it be
ſubiect, to the ragefull tẽpeſt of
the deuil againſt vvhich the vvic
ked being his inſtumentes, haue

D 5

combined togither, vvhofe puif-
fance and formidable attempts
vve cannot efchevve ; and therfore vvhofoeuer continueth
vvithin yt, muft liue in continuall vvarfare, and be fubiect to
many afflictionsand tribulations,
this is the courte of Iefus vvhere
the courtiers muft expect, no
greater fauour or priuiledge of
him, then all manner of afflictiõs,
and troubles, aduerfities and per-
Actoeum 5 fecution:for this caufe *ibant apo-*
ftoli gaudentes a confpectu concilii
quoniam digni habiti funt pro nomi-
ne Iefu cõtumeliam pati the apoftles vvent morecontented for ther
perfecutiõ,thẽ kinge Salomon to
be inuefted andcrovvned kinge of
Iuda:and vvhen the apoftle faith

ego Paulus vinctus in Dómino:holdeth him self more happie to be fettered in chaines for the loue of god,then if he had bene raised to the greatest principalitie of the earth.

For as in the pallace of princes, vvho is most fauored of the xinge,is best esteemed of the people: so in the house of god, his preferment is greatest, vvhome Chrieft doth most chastice, and ought to be put in the ranke of the chiefest friendes of god, vvho suffred Tobias to be blinded, Daniel t o be ymprisoned, Susanna to suffer sentence, not for ther harme, but to expresse the loue he bare them, this beinge one

proprietie in godes affection, to
chastice those, that he loueth, and
leaue others to ther destruction.
the perplexities that vve suffer,
for godes cause, thoughevve feele
them. yet god doth beare them:
and giues vs grace, and streingth
to indure them, if vvee suffer thē
for oure ovvne offences, or rather
for the trial of oure patiéce. they
ought rather to be called aduer-
tismentes, then punishmentes,
seinge they are corrections, to
amende vs, and not stumblinge
blockes to make vs stumble, nor
heauie burdens, vvhose vveight
may make vs fall, butt they be
furnaces necessarie, to refine oure
fayth, and instrumentes vvor-
kinge to our perfection.

This is the cause, that godlie people, are subiect, to manifold
afflictions. vvhen it is said *multæ*   *T.f.*
tribulationes iustoru. many tribulations are incident vnto the iust.

Dauid said *omnes fluctus tuos in-*   *Pſ.87.*
duxisti super me: all the traueiles
and dangers (oh lorde) vvhich
thoue vvert vvont equalie, to di-
stribuite, vnto others, thoue hast
novve reduced and returned op-
pon me onlye. Iob hauinge lost
his goodes, and his children, said
hoc sit mihi consolatio, vt affligens   *Iob. d.*
me dolore non parcas : greater consolation god could not send me,
then chastisinge my offences, to
spare no sortes of sorrovves vppó
me. *mihi absit gloriari nisi in cruce*   *ad Gal.6.*
Domini nostri Iesu Christi : I aske

no glorie faith fainct Paule then
to indure troubles, as by that
means to communicate vvirh the
glorie of Chrieft : holdinge it no
other glorie of this vvorlde, then
to be in continuall traueles, in
continual affliction, in conti-
nall aduerfities, all thiefe faith

2. ad Tmi
2. he : *fuftineo propter electos.* I fuffer for the elects fake togiue thē
example of patience in troubles,
by the exercife vvherof men be
com humble, and beinge often
tried they are the better iuftified
as the mettall that through many fiers, rifeth more to his fyne-
neffe and perfection.

Beleeue me and affure
youre felues, that if in patience youe receaue all youre

perplexities., youe shall receaue
youre revvarde vvithothers vvho
me god made happie by troubles, by vvhich ther patience vvas
tried, ther vertue increafed, and
ther fauour vvith god augmen-
ted:vvhofe examples vveare motiues vnto others to reforme
ther liues, to be forrie for ther offences paft : *& cogitare dies anti-* Pf. 76.
quos & annos æternos in in mente
habere, and to bethincke vvith
them felues there finfull dayes
paft in vvhich they haue deferued
the eternall and euerlaftinge
punishmentes that are due vnto
fuch grieuous finnes:if by temporall aduerfities,andaduertifmē-
tes they vvould not be reformed and reclaymed , and

beinge once moued vvith the cõ-
fideration of the horrible sinnes,
that vve haue so boldlie committed againſt god, and his lavves, as
Ezech. vvas vvhen he sayeth *reco-*
gitabo omnes annos in amaritudine
Vitæ meæ. vvhen I call to minde
hovv I haue miſpent my dayes
in follie, my life muſt be bitter
and yrckſom vnto me, vvee shal
find oure paines fare inferioure
to oure vvicked merites, and oure
offences rather touched, vvith a
mild iuſtice, then ſtrayned by
any due conection.

　S. Peter, after commitinge that
dolfull offence, againſt Chrieſt:
did thincke, all the punishmentes, that coulde be inflicted, too
litle, for him, and his eys vvere ne
uer

uer free from teares, the blessed
Marie Magdalin, esteemed 30.
yeeres pennanee in the vvilder-
nesse verye litle in comparison of
her offences: hauinge altogether
banished frõ her self, all vvordlye
delightes, that vvas the cause of
her fall. Dauid beinge strocken
vvith this consideration said: *Ecce
in flagellis paratus sum & dolor* Psal.37.
meus in conspectu meo semper: behold I am reddye for the vvhip,
and I hope I shall not vvant in
this vvorlde occasions to procure my grief, and to increase my
paine, the blessed apostle S.Paule
beinge reconciled vnto god
thought all the troubles, that he
sustained: verie light, in respect of
the sinnes that he hath commit-

E

ted.in nothinge did he glorie fo-
muche as in troubles, miferies, afflictions tribulations and bea-
ringeChriest his croffe, by vvhich
ad Gal. 6. (faid he) the vvorld vvas crucified vnto him, and he vnto the
vvorlde, of vvhom the prophet
pf. 38. fpeaketh: *hic eft ille vir cuius nomen Domini fpes eius & non refpe-
xit ad vanitates & infanias falfas,
&c.*this is he vvhofe hope is onlye fixed in god, and is not carried
a vvay vvith the vayne phantafies
and deceitfull alurementes of
this vvorlde: vvhofe onlye loue
is in the obferuation of godes
lavves : and vvhofe hearte is only occupied therin, and is not
blinded vvith couetuoufnes
nor ytched vvith ambition

vvhich may fay vvith the prophet
quid mihi eft in cœlo & a te quid *pl.38*
Volui fuper terram? Deus cordis meæ
& pars mea Deus in eternum (vvhat
shall I do in heauen vvithout
thee, much les haue I to do
vvith the earth. the god that
lodgeth vvithin my breaft
shalbe my portion for euer.
from vvhofe loue faith he
neyther perfecution, nor tribu-   *Rom. 8.*
lation, affliction, hunger fvvord,
death, principalitie, angell, man
deuill or vvorld, shal be able to alienat or eftrange my
hearte, for vvhofe fake he faid
mortificamur tota Die, &c. vve *pl.43*
be alvvayfe mortified and as
it vveare like sheepe ap-
pointed for the flaughter.

E 2

this is he, vvhich fought not like
a couard forChrieſt his fayth,and
vvas crovvned honorablie,by the
iuſt iudge for vvhoſe honoure,he
fought.this crovvne euerie one of
vs do ſeeke, and daylie pray for:
but vve cannot get the ſame butt
by a moſt ſerious combat againſt
fleaſhe, and bloode, and againſt
malignant ſpirits, and ther forces.

This bleſſedcrovvne cannott
be gotten, butt by thoſe meäns,
by vvhichChrieſt did ſet dovvne
Mat. 20. in his goſpel ſainge *poteſtis bibere
calicē*,can youe drincke of his cu-
pe?. can youe imitate his bleſſed
paſſiō,can you vvalke in the ſtrei-
cte,and harde vvay?can you beare
his croſſe, can youe deny youre

self? for as Chrysost. sayth *res pretiosa, non nisi, pretioso pretio comparatur*: none can reigne vvith Chriest vnlesse he imitat his passion. for a precious ievvel cannott be bought but vvith a precious price therfore as the blessed S. Paul saith *vigilate: state in fide, viriliter agite*, vvatch youre ovvne saluatio, hold fast your faith, behaue youre selues like stoute chāpions of Chriest, let all thinges be don according to charitie. remēber the firme purpose of christians, and behold the imageof Chriest crucified.

1. cor. 16

E 3

THE IVST ARE

Not forsaken of god althoughe, they seeme vnto the vvicked, to be most forlorne: and that in there greatest afflictions, they receaue of god the greatest consolation.

CHAP. III.

I T seemeth vnto Theodorus Beza, that Christ vtteringe thiese vvordes: *Deus meus, Deus meus vt quid dereliquisti me.* my

god my god vvhy haft thoue for-
faxen me? vvas in defperation and
out of all hope of confolation. it
feemeth alfo ftrange vnto the
Iues and gentiles, that Chrieft
beinge god , should be fub-
ie& , vnto the cruell , fierce,
and vnmercifull handes of fin-
ners. but it ought not to be
ftrange , that he , that came
to pay the debt of finne , yea
the finnes of all thevvorld, should
be punished as an vniuerfal
finner, forfaken of god if it
could be poffible, and of all the
vvhole vvorlde, and therfore the
apoft. faieth *qui non nouerat*
peccatum pro nobis peccatum fe-
cit, &c. Vvhich did not knovve
finne is becóme a ʒ finner

2.*Corin.* 5.

E   4

that is to saye suſtaineth the paine, that folovveth ſinne : and for all this repreſétinge not onlie the perſon of a ſinner: by vvhich he vvas vvorthye to be forſaken, but alſo the perſon of the iuſt, vvhich neuervvantes his comſorte in his greateſt tribulations: did beholde preſentlie the Angel Gabriel comfortinge him. god vvould neuer ſuffer vs to fight vvyth oure enymies, vvithout ſufficient forces and fightinge beholdeth vs, and in the ſkirmiſhe healpeth vs.

Chrieſt vvas preſent vvith Sanct Anthonie in the vvilderniſſe, fightinge vvith the deuill, althoughe he did not appeare viſiblie, vntill the deuill vvas van-

Luc 22.

D. Ath. in vita D. An

quished and S.Ant h.conquerou-
re. vvhich vvhen he asked of
Chrieſt,vvheare he vvas all this
vvhile. anſvveared that he vvas
preſent expectinge his inde-
uoure,and healpinge him in the
combate.

If god be pre ſent euerie vvheare,by his eſſence, preſence. and
povver (as he is in deede) accordinge to all the diuins,and accordinge vnto Mercurius Treſme-
giſtus, vvho ſayth that god, is *Mercurius Treſmeg*
figura ſphærica cuius centrum eſt
vbique circumferentia vero nuſquā:
god is a globe, vvhoſe centre is in
all places, vvhoſe circumference
is no vvheare:and as the prophet
ſaithe *ſi aſcendero in cælum tu illic* *Pſal.*
es, ſi deſcendero in infernum , ades: iſ

E 3

I aſcend vnto heauen there you
are:if I deſcend vnto hell : thou
arte preſent.

Actorum
capue 17.
If god be in all places and in
the entitie and beinge of euerie
thing,that he createth.asthe apoſt
le ſaith. *in ipſo viuimus mouemur &*
ſumus:in him vve liue, moue and
haue our beinge, vvhere fore
should not he be vvith theſe that
craue and implore his aſſiſtance,
as him ſelf auoutched by the prophet,and vve ought to beleeue
Pſal. 90.
him *clamauit ad me & ego exau-*
diā cum ipſs ſum in tribulatione, &c.
he hath cryed for my helpe:and I
vvill heare him , in tribulation I
vvilbe vvith him: I vvill deliuer
Act. 6.
and glorifie him.ſanct Steaue did
ſee him ſtandinge at the right hā-

de of the highest. he met S. Peter
goinge to Rome to be martyred.
and said thiese vvordes *vado Ro-*
mam iterum crucifigi. I go to Rome
to be crucified the second time
be cause, that S. Peter vvas goinge
thither to be crucified. as S. Am-
brose saith *in martyrio Christus oc-*
ciditur & in iis, qui pro fide patiũtur
aut mortē, aut vincula, aut verbera
Christi passiones sũt. &c. Chriest is
slayne in his martyrs, and vvho so
euer suffre death, fetters, stripes,
chriest suffereth vvith thē, that his
life may be manifested in there
death: vvherfore S. Paule desirous
of martyrdome sayeth *vivo ego iã*
non ego vivit in me Christus: though
I liue, yet it is chriest by vvhome
I ame quickned, that lues in me,

Abdias in
vita Sancti
peter.

amb. in 4.
c. 2 ad Cor.

ad Gal. 2.

vvhich giueth fortitude, and
ftrength vnto all martyts, vvhofe
fufferinge doth shevve the inte-
rance of the life to come, vvhich
Chrieft promifeth vnto them
that do fuffer tribulations for
his fake.

These afflictions of the iuft,
by vvhich ther patience, is exer-
cifed, andther grace increafed, are
great motiues to harden and confirme the vvicked in ther vngod-
lineffe.for beinge deliuered vnto
ther handes, theythinke that god
doth altogether forfake them,and
that he loueth them vvhome god
maketh his vvhippe, to fcourge
and punishe the godlie.and therfore the Turckes doe braggè, and
boaft, that they be the choyfen

people of god: for that be doth
vſe ther helpe to punishe the ſinnes of chriſtiãs, the hereticꝏes are
hardened and confirmed in ther
hereſies, by reaſon of ſo many victories gotten, by them againſt
catholicꝏes, vvhoſe manifolde
treſpaſſes, and horrible offences
haue giuen povver, and force vnto the aduerſaries, againſt them,
vvhich are ſuffered by god, to reforme the vvicked, and abhominable liues of catholickes, vvhoſe
miſeries, aud calamities: as they
ought to be a vvarninge to amẽd
the vices, and diſcompoſed beha
viour of the one: ſo they ought
not to be occaſions of the ruine
and obduration of the other.

aſſuringe your ſelues if ther re-

mayneth no finne amongeſt you
to be puniſhed:or negligence to
be chaſtiſed,or any fault to becor-
rected, yet your fayth muſt be
tried , by your patience:your religion made perfect by your perſecution : and god glorified, by
your tribulation *multæ tribulatio-*
nes iuſtorum the iuſt muſt be ſubiect to troubles and therfore let
none thincke,that your religion
is bad, becauſe it is perſecuted,or
you,that are the profeſſors therof,
to be forſake of god,becauſe he ſuf
fers you,to bethus perſecuted.the
vvife of Iob did more trouble her
husband the all his aduerſities. by
ſayeinge *ad huc permanes in inno-*
Iob. 2. *centia:benedic deo & morere.* your
innocencie giues you nothinge

els but death, praisinge god doth
purchase nothingee's for you but
tribulatiō: so Tobias for seruinge
of god deuoutlie, and for his tri-
bulatiōs by vvhich, he vvas tryed,
vvas reuiled by his vvife and friē- *Tob.c.3.*
des, vvho thought him to be most
cursed, andvnhappie as if god had
no care ouer such, as be in tribu-
latiōs: but the prophet sayth. *ocu li* *Psal.33.*
Domini super iustos & aures eius in
preces eorū god behouldeth the iust
and heareth t her cōplaint. the a-
postle declareth the same also: *in* *Cor.c.4.*
omnibus tribulatione patimur, sed non
angustiamur, a poriamur, sed non du-
struimur persecutionem patimur sed
non relinquimur: deiicimur : sed non
perimus : In all t inges vve suffer
tribulations, but vve are not per-

plexed, vve are as it vvere brought
ynto confusiō, but vve be not destroyed: vve suffer persecutiō; but
vve be not forsaken: vve be in the
brincke of all troubles: but vve
perishe not. because Christ for
vvhom you suffer, giueth you sufficient force to beare the burden

phil. 1.

of his crosse. *qui vobis dederat non
solum credere in eum: sed etiam pro
illo pati:* vvhich gaue you the grace: not onely to beleeue in him,
but also to suffer for him.

The

THE SERVANTE
Of Chriſt ought not to expeɛt
any true friendſhip of
this vvorlde vvhich is
the enimie of his maſter.

CHAP. IV.

A S. Chriſt, and this vvorlde are contrarie one to another: ſo are alſo there ſeruantes, and follovvers: ther vvorkes, and deſires, and beinge contrarie one to another, they can neuer poſſeſſe one kingdome:

F

muchleſſe reigne togither in one place. For vvhat communicatiõ can be betvvixt good and euill:vertue, and vice: light and darckneſſe:heauen and hell : god and the deuill.

2.Cor.6.

For no ſooner Chriſt, came vnto this vnthankfull vvorld, to redeeme it, from the ſlauerie of ſinne : from the captiuitie of the deuill , then he vvas reuiled, perſecuted, and banished of the ſame.

He vvas ſold in Ioſeph, he vvas ſlayne in the lambe, he vvas crucified in man , he vvas forſaken of the proude Ievves , that could not abide to ſee him. in a poore diſtreſſed ſtate; he vvas hotlie pur-

Gene.37.
Apo. 12.
Math.20,

sued of cruell Herod, that
stood in competencie vvith him
for the kingdome of Iurie.vvhich
vvas Chriest his right inheritance beinge rightlie descended,
from the tribe of Iuda,and from
the roote of Iesse, of vvhich,
through the blessed virgine he
tooke his humanitie, of Iudas he vvas sold, of his a-
postles he vvas forsaken, and
denyed,let vs not therfore mar
veile if you beinge the seruantes of Chriest the vvorlde
should hate, and detest you
for his sake, vvhich vvas euer
contrarie vnto him.It is not conuenient that vve should ioyne league or friendship-
vvith his professed enimie,

F 2

vvhose deceit is knovven , and vvhose treacherie is detected.

Let vs not forsake Chrieſt, thoughe vve fee him poore , hū-ble, perſecuted of manye and for-faken of all.

If Chrieſt came into this vvorl-de to edifie the people, to in-ſtruct them by his holie exam-ples, and to teache them vvhat they ought to do, vve ought to receaue his inſtructions. if po-uertie had not bene good, if the contempt of vvordlie honor had bene bad, he vvould not haue giuen vs examples, to embrace the one, nor counſell to defpiſe the other.

So as in his life vve fee him poore, bare, naked, and oppreſſed

vvith all afflictions and troubles,
vvhose examples ought to moue
vs. Vvee see that his gospell is
full of admonitions, and exhorta-
tions to forsake, and denye our
selues, to mortifie all our passions,
and not to conforme oure selues
vnto this vvorlde.

If Dauid to procure all his
subiectes to do pennance, that by 2.*Reg.75.*
that means gods vvrath shoulde
be appeased, and the people par-
doned, did ascend vnto mount
oliues, bare footed, and bare headed to the intente, the people
beinge moued vvith that example, should follovve him, and so
they did. if Alexander the great
in thevvarres of Persia (as *Quintus
Curtius* declareth) his armie

being muche troubled by the
abundance of fnovve, that fell
at that inftant, vvent him felf
a foote, and fo his armye by
his example vvent after, much
more ought vve to follovve
the example of Chrieft, and
to follovve his fteps, thoughe
vve fee him poore in this
vvorld and perfecuted of the
fame.

Iudi.9.   The prince Abimelech did
cutt a branche from a tree, and
did carrie the fame vppon his
ovvne shoulders, and commanded his foldiours to do the
like, and to follovve him : fo
Chrieft, the prince that vve
ought to follovve did beare his
croffe before vs to the end

that not only vve should beare,
but also follovve it , leaſt vve
should incurre the vvoe that is
pronoūced againſt such that bea *D. Ber.*
re thecroſſe and follovv not the
same *væ ſemel & væ iterum por-*
tantibus crucem Domini, & non ſe-
quentibus eam. Si Via crucis (as
Sanct Baſil ſaith) *in cælum patriam*
tuam te ducit, cur ab ea fugis
if the croſſe be your readie vvay
to bringe you vnto heauen:
vvhy should you flye from it?
and as Iſaias ſaith *Via tuta,* *Iſ. 26.30*
Via regia , Via certa , vt ſtulti *Pſal.118.*
non errent per eam. it is the *5. proues.*
readie vvaye , it is a ſafe
vvaye , and it is the κin-
ges high vvay , that fooles
cannot goe aſtraye therin.

F 4

this is the vvaye that Chrieſt
vvilled vs to follovve him. he vvēt
be fore vs bearinge his croſſe vnto mount Caluarie, vvhere vvee
behold him crucified, pitrifullie
vvhipped, ſtripped of his garmē-
tes, and leaſt naked, to increaſe
his paine and to augment his
ſhame, and confuſion, vvheare
vvee ſee him crovvned vvith
thornes, and nailed vnto a croſſe
of infamie, and malediction, vnto
vvhich they vveare ſubiect in
thoſe dayes that dyed after that
māner: vvhere (I ſay) vvee ſee him
depriued of all comforte and cō-
ſolation: beinge a ſpectacle of
ſhame and reproche vnto the
vvhole vvorlde.

Thus to follovve him I muſt

confeſſe is harde to be done to
fleàſhe and bloode: becauſe vvee
muſt fiſt learne to denye our
ſelues, forſake the olde mã I meane oure old humors of concu-
piſcenſe, mortifie oure ſelues, and
our vnreaſonable paſſions: caſt
of oure proper vvilles, and ſo take
vp his croſſe, and to beare patientlie all the aduerſities of this
vvorlde: and to ſuffer gentlie vvithout grudge all the deſplea-
ſant accidentes of this life.

If This bee the vvay of a Chriſtian vvhy ſhould he gape after
vaine honours of this vvorld and
follovve the lamentable pleaſures of this miſerable life.

If the capitaine Vrias vvould *2. Reg. 11.*
take no reſt at his ovvne houſe

F 5

for that the Arcke of our lorde
vvas abroad, vnder a pauilion.
vvhat reft can the feruantes of
Chrieft take, vvhen they behold
him nailed vnto a croffe. *Quam de*
D. Brens *forme eft* faith Sainct Bernard *fpi-*
nofo capiti habere delicatum mem-
brum. vvhat a deformed thinge
is it , that a head full of
thornes, should haue a delicate
member.

If the heade be troubled,
the reft of the members
cannot be at reft , but are
partakers of his paine , and
fubiect to his grief. If Chrieft
liued in continuall pouertie, in
continuall exile, in continuall
contempte of vvorldlye honours, hovve can vve hunt af-

.er promotions : gape for titles
of honours , and feeke riches. That therfore the members should agree vvith the
head , that the parte vvith
the totall , that the feruant be
conformable vnto his lord,
that the chriftian should embrace the example of Chrieft,
that the sheepe should ac
knovvledge the shepheard ,
that the prieft should offer him felf vnto him
to vvhome all facrifices are
offred . that the foldiour
should follovve the capitaine , that our bodie shoulde performe the vvill of the
fpirit and rhat the fpirit shoulde
accomplishe the vvill of god, vve

must conforme our selues vnto
his gospell and direct our liues
and actiõs accordinge to his bles
sed counsels, vvhich are nothinge els, then to beare his crosse, to suffer quietlie, and vvillinglie persecutions : to abide all
tormentes, rather then to viola-
te any of his commaundemen-
tes: to liue in continuall martyrdome for the felicitie of the
kingdome of heauen is giuen to
the poore in spirit and vnto such
that suffer for iustice and for the
testimonie of a good conscience
for accordinge to the apostle
omnes qui volunt pie viuere in Chri-
sto Iesu patiantur persecutiones: all
that intende to liue godlie in
Chriest Iesu, must suffer pesecu-

tions.for the vvorlde is not onlie
contrarie and oppofite to
euangelicall, and chriftian vertues but alfo to morall and
ciuil honeftie. becaufe it fauo-
reth but diffemblers and vicious
perfons.ther vvas a lavve amóge
the Atheniãs, that any, that had
done vvell for the common
vvealth, and liued vprightlie in
his actions, should be banished.
Ariftides beinge a man as vvell of
great deferts:as of a iuft and mo- *Plutar. in*
rall behauiour vvas punished *Vita Arift.*
according to this lavve : and
beinge demaunded of a blunt
commoner,vvhich did fubfcribe
vnto his banishmente,vvhat vvas
the caufe, that he did paffe his
fuffrage and verdite against fo

good a man: anſvvred that his
iuſtice vvas vngrateful vnto the
common vvealth and offenſiue
alſo vnto him.

　　So vnto men of vvicked
diſpoſitions, the good be yr
ckſome, and men of good life
be nothing acceptable. *conſide-*
rat peccator iuſtum, & quærit mor-
tificare eum : the ſinner doth
conſider the iuſt, and indeuo-
reth to ouertherovv him. If the
vvorld cannot abide men of
morall vertues. no meruaile,
if it cannot digeſt men of
ſupernaturall graces, and bleſ-
ſings vvhich muſt beare many
aſſaultes, contradictions, and
temptations therin. For the
ſcripture ſaith *fili accedens ad*

Pſal. 36.

Eccleſ. 2.

feruitutem Dei, &c. ſonne if thou
meaneſt to ſerue god, prepare and
arme thy ſelf againſt temptations
and troubles. the angel Ra-
phael ſaied vnto Tobias : becau- *Tob. 2.*
ſe thou haſt bene acceptable before god thou muſt needes be
tried, by temptations. God ſuffered this temptation to leaue
example vvith the poſteritie of
patience. Iob in his troubles ſa- *Iob.2.*
ied god doth trie me like golde.
God alſo did trie Abraham tou- *Gene.2 3.*
ching the oblation of his ſonne.
Iudith ſaith vnto the children of
Iſrael in the troubles of Ho-
lofernes , you ought to re- *Iudith.18*
member that god did trie our
fore fathers , vvhether they
loued him ſincerelie, or no

if thefe temptations had not
bin , Sanct Iames vvoulde not

Iac.1.   affirme them to be the caufe of
our greateft ioy.for bleffed(faith
he) that fuffreth them.for vvhen
he fhalbe proued by the he shall
receaue a crovvne of life vvhich
god promifed vnto all thofe that
loue him , Sanct Paul faith in

2. Cor.11   nothinge vvill I glorie but in my
infirmities and troubles : vnto
vvhich Sanct Frances faieth, he
vvas married.

For by the marriage , that is
contracted bevvixt Chrieft and
vs:vvee ought to affure oure felues that vve be married vnto the
afflictions of this vvorld.for in all
matrimonie the perfons contracted by reafon of the indiffoluble
knot,

knot, vvherin they be conioyned
and vnited are equallie partakers
of one anothers afvvell profperi-
rie, as alfo aduerfitie.

And feinge that the church *Eph 5.*
of vvhich you be members, vvas
vvedded vnto Chrift, vppon the
altar of the croffe (as the apoftle
fayth) this is a great facrament:
I fay in Chrieft and his church,
alfo in Sainct Iohn , come *Appo. 20.*
vvith me fayth the angel , and *21.*
I vvill shevve vnto you the vvife
of the lambe and he shevved vnto me the holye citie of Hierufalem , &c. and confequentlie euerie member of the church is ma-
ried vnto Chrieft as the fpoufe
faith in the canticles *dilectus meus* *Cau. 2.*
mihi & ego illi, &c. my beft be-
G

loued shalbe vvith me, & Ivvith him, vvhich is to be vnderstood of euerie faithfull soule, and as the apostle sayth.

2. Cor. 11 1ᵒ.

I haue married you vnto one man, to the end you should yeelde your selues a chast virgine vnto Chriest.

And seinge by this marriage, vvee are made partakers of all the merites, and treasures of Chriest his passion, vvhy should not vvee be also made partakers of his griefs, troubles, and persecutions : & seing our spouse by Isaias is called *vir doloi um* sayeng *non est dolor sicut dolor meus* : the mã of afflictions, there is no griefe so great as myne, for he vvas ouer vvhelmed vvith all kinde of sor-

Is. 53.

rovves, and tribulatiõs. he did sup
porte all our troubles, did suffer
all our miseries, and to make sa-
tisfaction for our offences, to ap-
pease the vvrath of the eternall
father against vvhõ the sinne vvas
cõmitted and the iniurie offered,
did paye the debt of sinne, & did
beare vppon his ovvne shoulders
the heauie burden of the punishmentes that vvee haue deserued
vvhich haue grieuouslie offen-
ded, and committed the same.

Let euerie one of vs beare his
portion of these miseries, let euerie one carrie his ovvne burden,
and euen as they be allotted
vnto vs: so sufficient grace, and
strength is assigned vnto vs, to
sustaine them.

Let vs follovve the spouse in
the canticles that said *ascendam in*
altum & apprehendam fructũ eius,
I vvill clime vnto the tree & ta
ke hold of the fruict therof : that
is to say the fruict of the noble
crosse, vvhich is nothing else thē
to entertaine vvillinglie all the
sharpe skirmishes of tentations,
to beare aduersities gentlie , to
punish our rebellious flesh:
and disordered desires, to embrace most heartilie all the austere vvorkes and trauailes of pennance, to bridle all the incoun-
ters, and vehement motions pro-
ceedinge from concupiscense
against reason, and our superiour
povvers : *& paruulos nostros ad pe-*
tram allidere : and to dash, and

Cãt. 7.

Psal. 136.

bruife oure litle vvhelps againft
the rocke, I meane oure vilde and
finifter tentations, and the dangerous fuggeftions therof, before
they be engendred by our vvilles, and hatched by our confent,
to ftop our malignant, and vene-
mous humonrs , to fuppreffe our
fenfuall inclinations, and appetites, to Keepe vnder the old man:
to put on the nevv : to chafe Is-
mael out of the houfe, that Ifaac
may poffeffe the inheritance of
his father , to crucifie our luxu-
rious carcafe , to mortifie our
members: and fenfes vvithall the
vices and concupifcenfe of the
fame: to the end that our fpirit
may enioy the patrimonie for
vvhich vvce are created, and re-

G 3

deemed, this is the vertue of chri
stian nobilitie, this is the continuall exercise of a christian life,
through this exercise the apostle
saith *mortificamur tota die prop-*
ter eum qui dilexit nos: vve are mor
tifieng of our selues for his sake

i Cor 9

that loued vs : this is the cause
that he chastised his bodie: *Casti*
go corpus meū & in seruitutem spiri
tus redigo carnem meam: I chastise
my bodie, and vnder the obedience of the spirite, I reduce my
fleash, and because in this mortification vvee are either negligent, or colde, others perhaps
vsurpe our charge vnto them
selues correctinge our slacknesse,
and chastisinge our negligence
and *nolentes cingi* and beinge vn

vvillinge to be girded, that is
to faye to fuffer for Chrieft or
abide any affliction, others novv
goe about to reforme vs,
& ducere nos quo noluerimus *Ioan.* 21.
and to lead vs vvhere vvee *Math.* 20.
vvould not, and beinge idle
in the market place, vvithout
any vvorke, or occupation, do
novve violentlie compell vs to
trauaile, and labour more earneftlie in Chrieft his vineyard, and
vvee beinge faint hearted, to encourage our felues, & being inf-
nared and intrapped in the briers and brambles of the vaine defires of this miferable
life, do conftraine vs to forfake
them, and beinge in the iavves
of the deuill, to deliuer vs

G 3

and our soule beinge full of the
rust of sinne, to clense, and purifie
it by the fire of tribulation.

A CHRISTIAN MVST
resolue vvith himselfe to fight
valiantlie against the eni-
mies of Chriest.

CHAP. V.

T is the parte of a
valiāt capitaine to
encourage his souldi
ors to the skirmish,
and   contemning
all dangers to propose vnto them

felues the revvarde of their labou
re taken in hand, and the crovvne
of the victorie expected, as alfo
on the other fide to fet before
ther eyes the bafe condition of
flauerie and bondage, in vvhich
they should haue bene if they
vvere ouercome, neyther onlie
the chriftians among the gentiles, but alfo Iudas Macabeus in
the battaile againft Nicanor, both
to encourage and embolden the
vveake and faint hearted, as alfo
to confirme, the ftrongeft, declared vnto theirs, againft vvhome
they fought, for vvhat caufe, and
to vvhat end. Told them alfo
that the victorie ftood not in
the multitude of foldiours, nor in
the furious affaulte againft vvho-

me they vvere to skirmish: but in
gods mightie povver, and that
they should not forget the manifolde dangers, out of vvhich
Mat 12 their anceſtors vvere deliuered,
and the vvonderfull victories
they had obtained, ſo that in that
battaile the Ievves did ouercome,
and their enymies vveare ouerth
rovvne hauing loſt 35.thovvſand
ſoldiers.euen ſo Chrieſt hauinge
triumphed ouer the povver of
darcknes, and ouer him, that had
the empire of death, hauinge
ſent his apoſtles as poore lambes
againſt tygres, lyons, and dragons
againſt the force of hell and tyrannie of man, did encourage
Ioan 14 them ſaieng : *non turbetur cor
veſtrum*: be not faint hearted:

for vvhen fuddaine feare , or apprehenfion, eyther of the danger
at hande,or of the euill to come
attacheth vs, then our fenfes by
the extremitie and vehemence
therof are difmaied, our foule is
vexed,and our heart trebleth for
feare , and therfore our fauiour,
biddeth vs to put greateftvvatch,
in the place of greateft danger:
and did ftrengthen vs by his ex-
hortations,and admonitions,that
vvhen the danger should come
vvee might be found valiant foldiers,that vve should not be like
the fish called Polypus , vnto
vvhich the Aegiptians did refem
ble fuch,as vvhen they be in any
great danger, or affrighted vvith
feare,are foone ouerthrovvne &

removed altogither from their
purpose: for vvhen that fish is
in any danger, it doth not flye or
prouide for safetie, but commeth
vnto the next banke and being
perplexed is taken by the fisher.
in these dangers of persecutions
let not any feare, or labour of
your trauailes, or loue of the
vvorld separate your heartes frō
Chrieft: but in all your dangers
and troubles say vvith the prophet: *bonum est mihi adhærere Deo*
& ponere in eo spem meam: it is
good for me to cleaue vnto god,
and to put my heart and affe-
ctiō in him, that vve may be able
to say vvith Sainct Auguftine:
amor meus: pondus meum. illuc feror
quocumque feror: that god beinge

Aeliau. de
Na hist li.
1.pcim. lib.
9. c. 29.

Psal.72

D. agu.

my loue:and my defire I may alvvaies dravve after him defpi-
finge any other thinge vvhat foe-
uer.Then vve fha be able to fay-
vvith the faid prophet:*fi confiftunt* Pfal. 26.
*aduerfum me caftra non timebit cor
meum.Si exurgat aduerfum me præ-
lium in hoc ego fperabo* : if all my
aduerfaries vvere in the field
againft me : my heart fhall not
be defmayed , if all the vvorld
vvould vvage vvarre againft me
therein I vvill hope to ouercome.

If vve Keepe not this lance of
god in our heartes by vvhich
vve may be holpen and defended againft the inuafions of malignant fpirits, againft the dangerous fuggeftions of the old

serpent:vvee shalbe compelled to
Psal. 72. say. *dereliquit me virtus mea, & lumen oculorum meorum nõ est mecũ:*
my forces do fayle me, and I haue
not the vse of my sight : and also
to say *defecit caro mea & cor meum·*
I haue no strength nor courage.

It is the parte of a constant
man in any great danger, or fierce shirmishe against his corporal enymies:not to be broken or
out of hart vvhẽ there is no remedie, to escape but by fighting,
much more a spiritual souldier
of Chriest ought not to retire
vvhen he is challenged to the cõbate, for the tryall of his fayth.
Heb. 13   then *optimum est gratia stabilire cor* : it is the best remedie vvee

haue to furnish our soule vvith *Heb.13.*
the grace and loue of god. For
fayth vvithout this grace and
charitie of god auaileth nothinge to vvithstand the eynmies thereof.

Vvee ought most earnestlie
vvith all humble and feruent
praiers to desire of god that,
vvhich he promised to giue by
Ezechiel: *dabo vobis inquit cor no-* *Eze.36.*
uum & spiritum nouum ponam in
medio vestri, &c. I vvill saith he,
giue vnto you à nevve hearte, &
a nevve spirit I vvill put amonge
you, that you may vvalke in my
precepts, and Keepe, and obserue
my ordinances.

In any great danger god neuer
faileth to giue nevve increase of

grace vvhich serueth not vnléfse it be put in execution, vvhen the re is occasion to vse the same.

In vaine is any force, or povver (as Arist. saith) vnles it be reduced vnto his operation, the talent of our lorde is idle, vvhē it is not increased by daylie profit, the fortitude of a valiant minde serueth to no purpose, vvhich in dāgers shevveth not his vertue, all motions are friuolous vnles they come vnto their end, the vvay is miserable that leadeth not vnto our cuntrie vvhich is heauen; in vayne vvee runne if vvee comprehend not Chriest, and of all men vvee be moft miserable, if vvee seeke for our laboures the revvarde of this vvorld. of vvhich

Chriest

Chrieſt did depriue his deereſt
friendes.

The onlie reſt, and felicitie vve
ſhould craue of god in this ſhor-
te life, is to prepare our heartes
for god, to direct oure vvorkes,
and vvills vnto him, and to diſ-
poſe, and frame our ſelues to ac-
compliſhe his bleſſed vvill, and
obey his commandement, as Dauid hath done *inclinaui cor meum* Pſ.
ad faciendas iuſtificationes tuas in
æternum. O lord I bind my ſelf for
euer to follovve, and obſerue thy
commandementes , to vvhich
purpoſe he ſaith *vnam petÿ a Do-* Pſal. 26.
mini, hanc requiram, vt inhabitem in
domo Domini omnibus diebus vitæ
meæ. one thinge I ſought of god,
and that I vvill earneſtlie craue

H

at his handes , that I maye re
mayne in the houſe of my god all
the dayes of my life vvhich is nothinge els then to dvvell in his
church , to abide in the arcke
vvith Noe, out of vvhich there is
no ſaluation , this is that arcke,
that although all the outragious
tempeſtes of perſecution, be ray-
ſed againſt it, is not drovvned: and
although all the povver of anti-
chrieſt be gathered to ouerthro-
vve it , remayneth ſtedfaſt , and
inuincible : and although all the
heretickes vvhich are the pirates
of the ſea, vvherein the ſame ſai-
leth, be cōbined together againſt
it, cōtinueth ſtedfaſt, and ympre-
gnable.

Bleſſed are your troubles if

you abide in the arcke, bleſſed is
your fayth, vvhen by the tryal of
perſecution novve intended, you
be found conſtant therin, bleſſed
is your religiõ beinge in your afflictions dulie obſerued, and in
your dangers perfectlye purified,
and bleſſed be your aduerſities,
that bringe patience, for tribulation vvithout exerciſe of that
vertue meriteth nothinge: vvhen
Chrieſt ſaith in your patiéce and *Luc.* 21.
not in your tribulations you ſhall
poſſeſſe your ſoules and enioy the
crovvne of your ſaluation. and S.
Cyprian ſaith *pæna non facit mar-
tyrē ſed cauſa:*torment maketh not
the martyre, but the cauſe for
vvhich he ſuffereth: and ſeinge
the cauſe of your troubles, is your

H   2

old anciēt faith:for vvhich as S.
Gregorie faith *luctamē cōtra malignos spiritᵒ fumeredebetis* you ought
to ftriueand ftruggle againft vvicked fpirits,you haue rather caufe
of cōfort,thē of forrovv;*quia merces veftra* as our fauiour faith *copio faᵢeft in cælis* be caufe your revvarde is great in heauen.

Ofeæ.2.

By this fayth Chrieft is efpoufed,and affianced in marriage (as) Ofee the prophet faith*defpūfabo te mihi in fide,& iuftitia.* I vvill betroth you vnto me in faith and iuftice. For by faith god dealeth vvith our foule,as a kinge that is to be married by his embaffadors,vnto a Queene that is abfente,vnto vvhich he fendeth his picture,that beholdinge and

feinge his proportion, and refem-
blance shee may loue him, and fo
accept of the marriage, and come
vnto him: this is the fame that the
apoftle fayth: *videmus nunc per ſpe-* 1. *Cor.* 13.
cuium in ænigmate tunc autem facie
ad faciem : vve behold him novv
as it vvere in a glaſſe or in obſcu-
rity, but thē in his ovvne kingdome , vve e shall contemplate him
face to face.

By fayth vve vvalke vnto him,
this is the fayth of vvhich the
apoſtle ſpeaketh, by vvhich (faith *ad Heb.11*
he) the ſainctes ovvercame king-
domes, they obtained ther defired purpofe, they haue ſtopped
lyons mouthes, they haue extinguished the furie of the raginge
fire , they vvere hardie , and

H 3

ſtronge in the battell, they haue
ouérthrovvne the forces of the
gētiles, ſome vvere quartered, ſo-
mé vvere caſt into priſõ, ſome vve
re vvhipped, and brought to cõfu
ſiõ, ſome vvere ſtoned to death, ſo
me vvere ſovvē in ſkinnes of beaſtes, and ſo caſt to be deuoured of
other beaſtes, ſome others did flie
vnto the moũtaines, vvhere they
ended ther liues in holes, incaues
of the earth in moſt pittifull mãner, in nakedneſſe and vvearines
theſe by the teſtimonie of their
faith vvere tried and by their trial
vvere found cõſtãte, and by their
cõſtácie leaſt behind thē bleſſed
exãples for vs to follovve; ſuch as
vvere good amõge the Iſraelits did
laboure in nothing ſo much as in

keepinge their fayth vnto god vn
ſpotted, & their religiōvndefiled.
this is the chiefeſt point in their
laſt teſtament to cōmitvnto their
childrē:this vvhen Ioſue vvas readie to die he did ſend for the tri-
bes of Iſrael reckoningvnto them   *Ioſue* 24.
ſo many priuiledges and graces
they had receaued of god and did
commend vnto them ſpeciallie
the obſeruation of his comman-
demēts,and a great zeale to hold
faſt their lavves. the like did old
Mathathias father of the Macabees
in the houre of his death , left no
other teſtament vvith his childrē,   *Maca.lib.*
then this hoalſome coūſell vvith   1. c. 1.
theſe memorabe vvoordes : chil-
drē hold faſt your lavves and giue
your liues for the teſtament of

youre fathers remēber the vvorkes, and exploites of your aūce-
tours vvhich they haue atchieued
and you shall obtaine immortall
glorie.

Att.ei.　S.Paul saith that he vvas not
onlie readie, to suffer and beare
all tormentes at Hierusalem, but
also to die for the name of
Chrieft: vvith vvhose loue, and
contemplation he vvas so much
rauished, that he saith so often
cupio dißolui, & eße cum Christo:
Gal. 2　I desire to be dissolued, and enlarged from the prison of this cor
porall lūpe, and to enioy Chrieft.
for vvhen he liued he said, *gaudeo*
in pasionibus pro vobis, & adim-
1.Col.1.　*pleo ea que desunt pasionum*
Christi, in carne mea prō corpore

eius quod est ecclesia: I reioice in
sufferinge for you, and do ac-
complih vvhat vvanteth of
Chrieft his paffions in my flesh,
for his body, vvhich is hischurch:
not that there vvas any thinge of
Chrieft his paffion or the merites
therof left vnfinished (for he hath
sufficientlie satisfied the eternall
father *de rigore iustitiæ*, as the di-
uines doe say in the rigour of iuftice for our offéces) but the afflictions, and tormentes that the
sainctes do suffer for the church;
should be added, and ioyned vnto
Chrieft his sufferance, and paffion to increase, and augment the
treasures of the churche, for the
alayég and affvvaginge the dread
full paines, due vnto our sinnes

out of vvhich treatures and riches
so many indulgences are granted
by the chief pastor therof for this
purpose:vnto vvhich agreeth the
glose of S. Ambrose vppon that
place. *suppleo reliquias pressu
rarum Christi in carne mea pro corpore eius quodest ecclesia.* I do make
vp the relickes and fragmēts that
lacked of the passion and tormentes of Christ in my ovvne
fleshe, vvhich is his church. the
consideration vvherof moued. S.
D.Basil. Basil before the iudge of the Emperour threatninge and cōman-
dinge him vnder paine of death,
to forsake his olde religion ; and
to conforme him self vnto the iniū-
ction of the Emperoure, to
saye:I vvould I had a better gift

to be reprefented vnto him, that
vvould deliuer me out of this
corrupte carcafe, out of this chaos
of confusion, out of the valley of
teares, and out of the shadovv of
death: then this poore life of mine vvhich god did léd vnto me to
ferue him : and novve this is the
time that I ought to offer it in a
liuelie facrifice for his honoure
that gaue it and for his church.

S. Paule alfo vvritinge vnto the
Romans *obfecro vos* faith he *vt ex-* **Rom. 12.**
hibeatis corpora veſtra, hoſtiã fanctã
Deo placentẽ, rationabile obfequium
veſtrũ noḷte cõformare huic feculo:
I defire you moft earneftlie, that
you offer vp your bodies a liue
lie and holie hofte in a moft fer-
uiceable and pliãt mãner vntogod

vvhich muſt be gratefull and acce
ptable vnto him: anddo not cófor
me your ſelues vnto this vvorlde.

The reaſon vvhy vve should ſo
do, he giueth vnto the Corinth:
2 ad Corin.
c.5. ſaieng *Chriſtus pro omnibus mor-*
tuus eſt, vt & qui viuunt non ſibi vi-
uant ſed ei qui pro ipſis mortuus eſt,
& reſurrexit : Chrieſt vvas dead
for all, to the ende, that ſuch asdo
liue, should not liue vnto them
ſelues, but they should liue, and
die for his ſake, vvhich vvas dead
and did riſe for them.

Moſt noble chriſtians deſcen-
dinge from the loynes of Abraham, from the familie, and race of
Iacob, from the ſtocke of Ieſſe,
from the victorious and trium-
phant lyon of Iuda, like noble

lyon behaue your felues in this
combate of your faith, in vvhich
if you shrinke and shevve your
felues bafe and couardlie foldiers
(vvhich god for bid) it is not the
temporal feruitude of 7, or 100,
yeares or, that of men, vvhich
though they be neuer fo cruell
haue fome commiferation, or fome kind of humanitie tovvardes
one another, but it is the perpetuall, and moft miferable flauery
and captiuitie of deuils, vvhich
hath no pitie, or compaffion of
man, that you do hazard and
purchafe vnto your felues, neyther is it an Earthlye kingdome,
or temporall inheritáce you loofe thereby, but the euerlaftinge
glorye of paradice, the focietie of

the bleſſed ſainctes the conſolation of Chrieſt and the viſion of
the bleſſed trinitie vvherin conſiſteth all oür felicitie, remember
vvhat ouerthrovv your faith hath
giuen vnto all the forces of Sa-
than, andvvhat glorious victories
it hath gotten againſt all the
vvorld. as S. Iohn ſaith *hæc eſt vi-*

I. Io.5   *ctoria, quæ vicit mundum : fides*
veſtra, by your ſayth the victo-
rie is gotten againſt the vvorlde.

Be not carried avvay vvith
the falſe reſemblance of the vn-
conſtant promotions of this
vvorld, caſt of all the vayne hope
of the dangerous honoures of
mortall men: *accipite* as the apoſt-
ad Eph.6. le ſaith *armaturam Dei, vt poſſitis*
reſiſtere in Die malo. putt on the

complete harnesse of god, that
you may resist in the euill day.

Imitate the lyon, vvho beholdinge the hunters comminge
verie stronge against him, and
beinge not able to shunne them,
respecteth not their strength,
nor their vveapons, least hee
should be terrified therby, beholdeth onlie the earth and stri-
keth him self vvith his taile:
euen so in all our difficulties
vvee ought to beholde our
frailtie, and proper miseries,
and the shortnesse of oure temporall life, so vncertaine, so oppressed vvith sundrie calamities
vvherin the banished and forlorne children of Eua doe lye
hovvlinge, and groueling,

vvhich are deformed vvith so
many spottes, and blemishes of
disloyaltie, and dissobedience
against god, troubledvvith so many passions, distracted vvith so
many cares, confounded vvith so
many errors, ouervvhelmed vvith
so many temptations, altered
vvith so many humoures, infected vvith so many diseases, ex
posed vnto all dangers of eternall
vvoe, if our soule be corrupted
by sinne, and not replenished, or
beautified by the grace of god,
or not mortified, by the rod of
discipline, or not hated of such as
before did loue it, for as Christ
saith: *qui odit animam suam in hoc*
mundo, in vitam æternam custodit
eam, &c.

Luc.14,
10,12.

vvho

vvho hateth his life in this vvorld
shall preferue it vnto life euerlaftinge.

Accordinge to S. Aug. *ſi male
amaueris tunc odiſti, ſi bene oderis
tunc amaſti, fœlices qui oderunt cu-
ſtodiendo ne perdant amando:* if thou
loueft it ill: then thou hateft it: if
thou hateft it vvell; then thou
haft loued it, and bleſſed are
they that hate it, by keepinge it
leaſt they loofe it, by louinge it.
certainely he that hateth it is
he that ouercometh the fearefull
pangs of the ſecond death: It is
ſaid: *qui vicerit non lædetur a morte
ſecunda.* vvho foeuer ouercom
meth shall receaue no harme
of the ſecond death, and shall alſo receaue the inuiſible and hiddē

*D. Aug.
tract.51.in
Ia.*

*Apoc.*2

I

māna and seinge our ovvne forces are so slēder and our aduersaries so innumerable and so strōge
as vvee are not able to ouercome
them, but by supernaturall heal-
pes and graces, that our heartes
may be inflamed vvith his loue
and inkindled vvith blessed desires, that vvee may say vvith the

Psal. 38. prophet *concaluit cor meum intra
me* my heart did vvax vvarme in
my bodie and vvith. S. Aug. *scribe
domine vulnera tua in corde meo vt
ibi legam dolorem & amorem &
cuncta aduersa propter te sustineam li
benter.* O lord vvrite thyvvoundes
in my hearte that therin I may
beholde vvhat loue youe doe
beare vnto me and troubles you
suffred for me, and vvill embrace

all aduerfities vvillinglie for thy fake. and fo I vvill neuer feare *in domine fperaui nontimeboquid faciet mihi homo* vvhat man can do againft mee. *Pfal.55.*

TO BEGINN VVEL,
and not continue therin
auaileth nothinge to our iu-
ftification.

CHAP. VI.

GOD promifed vnto vs, a revvarde for our la-boure, a paye for our vvorke and a crovvne for the victorie, vvhich neyther

I 2

he vvill beſtovve more vve ſhal re
ceaue, vntill our vallour be knovven, and the battell ended,
vvhich beginneth againſtvs, vvhẽ
vvee haue the vſe of reaſon, vvhẽ
vvee beginne to manage and diſ-
poſe our actions according or
contrarie to reaſon, and continueth vnto the laſt momẽt of
our life.

Our ſauiour telleth vs *qui per-*
Math. 24. *ſeuerauerit vsque in finem hic ſaluus*
erit: vvho ſo euer ſhall perſiſt vnto
the end ſhalbe ſaued if vvee be
faithfull in our promiſe made
vnto god, and patient in our laboures ſuſtained for him, he alſo
vvilbe faythfull and vndoubt
full in accompliſhinge that he
promiſed : liberall and boun-

tifull in revvardinge vvhat vvee
haue deserued.

This is it vvhich he said spea- *Luc.* 2 2.
kinge vvith his disciples you are
those that do abide vvith me in
my troubles and temptations,
and therfore I haue determined
to giue vnto you a kingdome: he
said fellovves and partakers of his
trauailes and therfore of his ioy
in his kingdome.

To begine to be godes seruant
proceedeth of the grace of god
but to continue therin vnto the
end of our liues a special grace
and blessing of god vvith many
infused and supernatural vertues
are required, and chieflie a constant hearte that no perturbation
bee able to make it recoile

I 3

from his dutie in such manner as
by no temptation itvvaxeh faint,
or by importunitie of trauell he
forbeareth to do good.

Of this vertue S. Anthonie and
S. Hylarie vveare great and holie
examples vvho suffred great
tentations in the desarte and yet
did not forbeare to do god great
seruice.

Lucius Seneca doth attribute
so much to the excellencie of a
man heartie and valiant that he
maketh it harder to vanquish a
mind inuironed vvith the vertue
of conftancie:then to take a cittie
vvel fensed and guarded.

In Epla. 　S. Hierom *faith per bonam & ma-*
lam famam a dextris & a finiftris
miles Chrifti graditur,&c. no other

thing is the paſſage of this life,
then a publicke vvay on vvhoſe
rigt hand marched the valiant
and hardie man, on the left parte
the couarde and faint hearted,
and betvveen them both goeth
the ſtronge ad reſolute. and accordinge to S. Gregorie *fortitudo*

iuſtorum eſt carnem vnicere, proprijs **li. 8. mor.**
voluntatibus contraire , delectatio-
nem vitæ preſentis extinguere: huius
mundi aſpera pro æternis præmijs
amare proſperitatis blandimenta con-
temnere, aduerſitatis metum in cor-
de ſuperare : the fortitude of the
iuſt is nothinge els then to maſter the fleaſhe, to reſiſte the appetits of our proper vvil, to extinguish and deſpiſe the delights
of this life, to affecte thinges of

I   4

hard enterprise for the kingdome
of god, not to be carried avvay,
vvith the vaine alurementes of
vvorldly vvealth, and not to es
chevvsuch as be both painfull and
perilous.and asOrigines saith *sicut*
continens vita, labor, perseuerantia,
& agonum certamina faciunt vnum
quuemque virum virtutis appellari: sic
e contrario; vita remiſſa, negligens, &
ignaua facit virum ignauum iudica-
*ri:*euen as a man of a continent
life, toylſom laboure, and of per-
ſeuerance in a dangerous doubtfull battell deſerueth to be reputed a vertuous man:ſo on the con
trarie ſide a man careleſſe, negligent, and ſluggish, is holden for a
couarde. this is the vertue vvithout vvhich no heroicall deſi-

Orig. ſup.
lib.numerū
hom.5.,

gnementes can be perfourmed
and vvithout vvhich vvee ought
not to be holden for chriftians:
for the character by vvhich vvee
be called by that name, auayleth
vs nothinge, vnles vvee perfift
ftill and perfeuer vvith Chrieft.
Iudas reapes no profit for beinge
one of oure fauiours apoftles becaufe he did not continue vnto
the end: For the good lucke,
and skill of an expert pilot confi-
fteth not altogither, to guidevvell
the helme, but rather that he
bringe it to arriue fafe at the ha-
uen:euen fo Chrieft promifeth
not the kingdome of heauen to
fuchonlie, as are baptifed nor to
him that is called a chriftiã, if he
perfeuere not in his feruice, for

I 5

the crovvne of the triumphe, is
not beftovved vppon him that
goeth vnto the vvarres : but is
vvourthilie referued forfuch as
obtaine the victorie. although the
fierie columne conducted the
children of Ifrael out of Aegipt:
yet it did not bringe them to the
land of promife. fo as none did
enter into the fame but fuch as
did in firme hope perfeuere vnto
the end of the battell ; by vvhich
they ouercame their enimies,
and fo obtained the victorie, and
gained the defired land : the laboure of Nehemias and Efdras
after retourninge from the captiuitie of Babylon vvould be fru-
ftrated in buildinge the temple at
Hierufalem , if iniuries, threat-

Num. 14.
Exod. 13.

ninges, ftronge enymies vvhich
had all their forces bent againft
them, vvould haue eyther terrri-
fied them from making an end, or
perfvvaded them to giue over
and trulie your chriftianitie, and
catholicke religion shall rather
procur your damnation, then in
any manner helpe yon to iuftifi-
cation, if eyther for feare of man,
or loue of the earthe, or any danger of perfecution you giue it
ouer or be inconftant therin : if
it vvere to gaine the vvorld, or to
faue oure life, vvee ought not to
cõmit one deadlie finne, or tranf-
greffe the leaft of godes commã-
dements, much leffe to make a
ship vvracke of oure faith and religion, vvhich vvee ought to de-

Ephes.3.a.8

fend vvith.loffe of life and goodes, if vvee be called in queſtion
for the fame. If the godlie vvo-
mã Snſanna vvould rather fuffer
death then yeeld vnto the exe-
crable luſte of the vvicked iudges,
that follicited her to defile her-
bodie, if a valiant captaine, and a
gratious matrone ought to ſuffer
death, rather then to committe
treaſon:the one againſt his kinge,
the other againſt her married
busbãd.much more ought vve to
ſuffer all extremities vvhatſoeuer
then to committe treaſon againſt
god by forſakinge him, and his
church for vve be more obliged
vnto him and his church, then
eyther the captaine vnto his
kinge 'or the vvife vnto her

hufband.

Let vs therefore abide vvith
god and not fuffer our felues to
be feparated from him:let vs cō-
tinue in his catholicke church
out of vvhich vvee can neyther
ac knovvladge,loue,or ferue him,
let the end of our labour and per
feuerance in his religion to the
laft moment of our liues bee a
fufficient vvitneffe of our loue
to vvardes him,and an euident ar
gument to his church of our
faith and religion.the laborer in
the gofpel vvas not revvarded
vntill the vvorke vvas finished,
nor torment or paine could
vvithdravve Chrieft from the
heroicall vvorke of our redemp-
ption vntil the eternall father

vvas by his paſſion ſatisfied for
our offences and vvee miſerable
ſinners redeemed from the thral-
dome of the deuill. this ſufferan-
ce and paſſion of Chrieſt auaileth
nothinge vnto vs, vnles vvee follovv him and continue vvithim
vnto the ende as S. Peter ſaith
chariſſimi, Chriſtus paſſus eſt pro
nobis, vobis relinquens exemplum,
vt ſequamini veſtigia eius : moſt
louinge Chrieſt did ſuffer for vs,
leauinge vs example to continue in the profeſſion of our faith
vvhich vvhen he deliuered vnto
vs, did ſuffer all difficulties and re
proches vnto the infamie of the
croſſe. The kine that did carrie
the arcke of our lorde, althoughe
ther calues vvere bellovvinge

1. Pa.2.

behind them, they neuer retour-
ned or vvent on the right fide or *1. Reg.c.6.*
the left, but vvent directlie for
vvarde vntill they came vnto the
land of Bethfamis: euen fo vvee
that carrye the croffe of Chrieft
vppon our shoulders ought neuer to leaue it of, thoughe our
fenfible appetites vvould cry vppon vs, to leaue it of, vvhile vvee
arriue at the land of reft. The
beaftes that Ezechiel did fee did *Ezech.c. 1*
direct their courfe, vvhere the fpirit moued them, and neuer retour
ned backe. If the vvoman of Lot
had gon forvvard vvithout tour-
ning her head backvvard, she
had not bene tourned vnto an
image or ftone of falt: gods commandement vnto her, vvas to go

A M nemosynum to the alvvaies for vvard vvithout looking backe. *Nemo mittens manum ad aratrum, &c.* none puttinge his hand to the plovve and aftervvardes looking backe againe is apt for the kingdome of heauen. If once vvee purpose to be the seruantes of god, and to continue as his adoptiue children vvithin the arcke of his churche, vvee should neuer forsake so blessed a purpose nor suffer our selues to be cast out of so sure and so certaine a place, If Adam in originall iustice vvould haue persisted, neyther had he bene thrust out of paradice, nor vvee subiect to so many miseries and tribulations. If Salomon vvould haue perseuered in the fauour so abõdantlie

dantlie receaued of god, his falua
uation had not bene fo doubtfull : if the firft angel and iudas
had continued as they began, the
one had not bene thruft out of
heauen, nor the other depriued
of the apoftleship, nor of all the,
fruite and merite of his former la
bours. if Moyfes and Aaron had
not giuen ouer their hope to obtaine the land of promife, they
had entred therin vvith Iofue
and Caleph. many men had great
fauours of god: but becaufe they
vvanted the bleffed gift of per-
feuerance, vvhich is nothing els
then a continuation in the good,
& gods gratious fauour vnto the
laft gafpe of our liues , thofe fauours ate nouv rather an increafe

K

of their vvoe, then a diminishing of their euerlasting paine.
And therfore the councell saith *Adiutorium D i & renatis & sanctis simpliciter est implorandum vt ad finem bonam peruenire possint:* euerie one, though neuer so holic and of god adopted, must simplie, and sincerlie implore his speciall healpe, that he may come to a good end. *ad quacumque partem ceciderit lignum siue adaustrum siue ad aquilonem ibi manebit:* vvheare soeuer the tree falleth, vvhether it be tovvardes the South, or North, there it remayneth, if vvee dye in gods grace vvee shalbe sure to obtaine glorie, though vvee may be in purgatorie vntil the paine due vnto the sinne be

Conc. Trid.

c Ecclef. 11

satisfied, if vvee die in deadlie sin
ne, ther is no hope of faluation,
nor of the inheritance purchased
for vs by the blood of Chrieft,
vvhich vve ought vvith feare and
tremblinge to procure , being
not affured therof, vvhen it is
faid *nemo fcit vtrum odio vel amore*
dignus fit : none Knovveth vvhether he be vvorthy eyther of
loue or of hatred, and as Iob faith
fi venerit ad me non videbo eum , fi
abierit non intelligam : vvhen god   *Iob.9*
vvill vvouchfafe to come vnto
me, I shal not perceaue it , and
vvhen he vvill departe from me
by his grace, I shal not vnderftãd
it, vvherfore faith he. *fi fimplex fue*
ro hoc ipfum ignorabit ánima mea: If
I be fimple it is vnKnovven vnto

me and therfore S. Paule sayth
nihil mihi conscius sum sed in hoc nō
iustificatus sum although my cō-
science doth not accuse me, yet
I am not therby iustified, because
as the prophet saith *peccatum con-*
tra me est semper my sinne alvvaies
opposeth it self againſt me. Therfore in a bodye so corrupt, so enfeebled vvith sēsualities, in a soule so subiect vnto sinne, in a ſtate
so ful of temptatiqns, in a vvarfare againſt so dangerous an hoaſt,
so mightie and so strōge, as there
is no povver vppon the earth able to reſiſt it, vvithout the special
grace of god: for vvhich reasōs let
a man be neuer so iuſt, he is not
aſſured of his saluation *niſi perſe-*
uerauerit vsque ad finem vnleſſe he
endure vnto the ende.

THE VERTVOVS,
and godly people muſt haue aduerſaries in this world.

CHAP. VII.

NO cauſe canvvorke vvithout a ſubiect, and vvhen the vicious and vvicked are certaine morall cauſes, that vvorke according to their malice : For as Ariſtotle ſaieth no cauſe can vvorke but in a côtrarie principle and therefore *contra bonum, malum: cѕntra vitam. mors:* Euill vvorketh againſt good

Ariſt lib. pri. phiy. c. 5. & 7.

K 3

Pſal. 18

death againſt life. *Circumueniá-
mus iuſtum (loquuntur impÿ) quoniam contrarius eſt operibus noſtris,
& diffamat nos:* Let vs intrap the
iuſt man(ſay the vngodly)becau-
ſe he is contrary to our doinges,
and doth diſcredite vs.

Vertue is a certaine qualitie of
the mind, vvhich is oppoſite to
vice, and can neuer be produced,
but by contrary qualities, by
vvhich all other qualities are ingendred: So that if in earth ſo
many bloody tyrants had not
raigned, ſo many bleſſed Martyrs had not triumphed in heauen, the vertue of vvhoſe patience exceeding the violence of per
ſecution, hath gained ſpirituall
riches to the church, & a crovv-

ne of glor ie to them selues.

This contradiction betyveen
vertue, and vice continued
from the beginning. No sooner
came man into this vvorld, but
the deuill defied him, as an ene-
my. The firſt tyvo brethren, A-
damschildren prefigured this, the
one ſo ſetting himſelfe againſt
the other, that hee ſlue him becauſe him ſelfe xvas not ſo good.
The ſeed of this diſcorde tooke
roote in Iacob, and Eſau ſonnes
of Iſaac, Eſau being a type of the
vvicked, and reprobate, repining
at Iacob in vvhom the elect, vye-
re figured; & as Sainct Auguſtin
said. *Sicut duo paruuli in vtero* Gen.23 &
25.
Rebeccæ: ſic in vtero eccleſia duo ſibi
populi inuicem aduerſantur. Euen

K 4

as the tvvo infants contended in
the vvombe af Rebecca so tvvo
sortes of people do striue, &
struggle togither in the body of
the church. But vvhat should I
recount the controuersie of contrarie natures, that is to say of
man, and an Angell, or of diuerse
persons borne both of one mother, & nourished perhaps vvith
one milke as of Abel, and Cain,
Iacob and Esau, or the enmitie
of other people, some fighting
vnder the standard of god, some
of the deuill: Ioseph vvas sold by
his enuious brethrē, Dauid perse
cuted by lunaticke Saul, Elias pur
sued by vvicked Iezabel, Elizeus
mocked by vngodly children,
Ierusalem brént by proud Nabu-

chadonofor, and Sufanna flande-
red by tvvo adulterous iudges. In
all this note that the iuſt had ſome ſingular vertue, the vniuſt
ſubiect to ſome notorious vice,
But vvhat should I recount
theſe contentions of diuerſe natures in diuerſe perſons, vvhē the
very ſame is foond in man being
but one perſon, or one ſubiect?
For the like contention vvas neuer ſeene betvvixt ennimies as is
daily betvveene the tvvo eſſētiall
partes vvhereof man is cōpoſed,
& made; I meane the ſoule, and
thebody, the ſpirite, and the fleſh
the ſuperiour, and inferiour partes; inſomuch as the life of the
one, is the death of the other, the
food of the one the poiſon of the

K 5

other, the gaine of the one the
losse of the other, and in breefe
the vveale of the one the vvoe of
the other: And from hence it pro
ceedes, that vvee stand in need of
so many graces, and vertues,
vvhich albeit they are conferred
vnto vs in the holie Sacrament of
Baptisme: yet the soule cannot
vvithout much difficultie exercise them by reason of the contradiction of the bodie, vvhereas if
the soule vvere at libertie, it
might make vse of them vvith
great facilitie. And in goodsooth
it is no marueile, that carnall
people do so much contradict,
and oppugne the lavv of grace,
vvhich is a spirituall lavv, if the
flesh(being so vnited, and ioined

to the spirite(that of thē both one humane nature resulteth)doth so eagerly pursue the spirit, and vvith so much despite,that to destroy it, shee feares not to be her ovvne destruction. Euen as Sainct Paul saieth. *Littera (id est) caro occidit.* The flesh doth Kill, vvhich enmitie is also verified in Isaac and Ishmael,the sōne of the bondvvoman vvhich vvas borne according to the flesh, daring to mocke,and deride the freeborne Isaac,vvhose natiuity vvas according to the spirit.

And therfore the gospel of Iesus Christ being spirituall vvas vvith such vehemence impugned : For against it the Roman emperours bēte all humane forces, against it

1 Cor. 5

Gal. 4
Gen. 21

the philosophers opposed all
vvordly vvisedome, against this
carnall people vvallovving in sinne and concupiscēce and loth to
leaue their delightes, made insur-
rection, also that great Dragon
raised all his povver. *Aduersus il-*
lud principes conuernerum in vnum:
Against it the Kings of the earth
combined them selues, against it
first all pagans, aftervvards all
Heretickes, and Schismaticxes
conspired: *Videns diabolus* (saieth
Zealous Sainct Augustin) *dæmo-*
num templa deseri & in nomen libe -
rantis mediatoris & currere genns hu
manum, hæreticos monit quisub vo-
cabulo Christiano doctrinæ resisterēt
Christianæ. The deuil seing his tē-
ples to bee left, and all thē vvorld

Apoc 12.
Psal. 2. a

august. de
cā uit. dei li
8 cap.52.

run to embrace the svveet name
of their redeemer, and mediatour
stirred vp the Heretickes, vvhich
vnder the title of chriſtians
should oppose them selues to the
chriſtian doctrine. *Per verba legis* ᴵⁿ ᶜᵒⁿ. ᵃⁿ
legem impugnant (ſaith Sainct Am- ᵀᵏ.
broſe) By the very vvordes of the
lavv they reſiſt the lavv. Nay but
the Caluiniſtes profeſſe faith alſo
but Sainct Hillary tels them : *Fi-*
dem ſine fide pratendunt, that they ᴵⁿ *litura*
pretend ſaith vvithout faith. The
pſalmiſt anſvvereth them. *Molliti* ᵖˢᵃˡ.54.
ſunt ſermones ſuper oleum, & ipſi
ſunt iacula. That their vvords are
ſteepe d in oile, but indeed they
are dartes. *Venenum aſpidum ſub* ᵖˢᵃˡ. 139
labiis eorum. That the poiſon of
Adders is vnder their lips. *Ve-*

niant ad vos (saith our blessed sauiour *in vestimentis ouium intrin-*
secus autem sunt lupi rapaces. They
come vnto you in sheepes clo-
thing, but in their hartes they are
rauening vvolues : to vvhich
saieng blessed saint Bernard allu-
ding, telleth some of them that
they are, *Foris candidi, intus autem*
sordidi: Though out vvardly they
seeme as vvhite, as snovve, yet in-
vvardly they beare another hue.
small difference Sainct Augustine, putteth betvvene Pagans, and
Heretikes: *Persequitur paganismus*
(saith hee) *aperte, sæuit vt leo, hæ-*
reticus insidiatur vt Draco : Paganisme persecuteth the church
openly, and roreth like a *Lyon,*
but thé hereticke lurketh as a

Dragon:The one compelleth to
deny Chrift, the other teacheth
the fame, the one, vfeth violence,the other treachery,vve muft
be patiét for the one, & vvatch-
full for the other. Thus much
faith Sainct Auguftin in the
peaceable time of the church.
By vvhofe admonition vvee are
taught hovv vvee should behaue
our felues in thefe dangerous
daies,leaft our function should
bee contemned, and fimple Ca-
tholicks fcandalized, vvhich
may be an occafion of their
ruine, & a prouocation of gods
vvrath againft vs,if through our
negligence they vvould be care-
leffe of their faluation. Therfore
S. Peter bideth vs to vvatch *quia*

A Mnemosynum to the *aduersarius noster diabolus tanquam leo rugiens circuit, querens quem deuoret* becaufe our aduerſarie (faith he) the deuill like a roaringe lyon goeth a bout ſeeking vvhom he may deuoure.

✠✠✠✠✠✠✠✠✠✠

THAT THE CHVRCH
of god frõ the beginning vvas
perfecuted , and againſt
Chriſt the head this perfe-
cution vvas intended.

CHAP. VIII.

I Vvil (ſaith Chrieſt) ſend vnto you pro- phets, and Apoſtles, vvhich ſhalbe both Killed and perſecu- ted, vvhich falleth out as Chriſt foretold ſpeakinge vnto his A- poſtles *preſſuram in mundo habebi- tis,* you ſhalbe tormented in this

Luc.c.11.
Mat.5.14
Ioh.15.&
16.

L

vvorld: the deuill euer ftirreth vp
his vvicked miniftets to deftroy
the church of god but cheifly
the paftors as the principal parts
ther of:Alexander the great vvhē
he did befiege Athens faid, that
his quarrel vvas not againft the
citie,but againft the ten orators,
that vvere vvithin,vvhich if they
vvere deliueted into his hands,
he vvould raife the feige,and ioi-
ne a nevve league of freindship
vvith the Citizens, for all his
quarell as he faid, vvas againft
thofe orators,vnto vvhichDemo-
ftenes replied after this manner.
The vvolues did fpeake after this
fort vnto the sheapehards, all the
difcord that is betvvixt you andvs
proceedes of your dogs, & if you

plutar: in
vita ；eiue.

vvill deliuer thē vnto vs, vve vvil
be perfaict freinds. The dogs
being rendred vnto them , and
peace eftablished , the vvolues ro
fe vpon the poore flocke,and deftroied it : euen fo Hereticxes in
thefe daies goe about to taxe
avvay religious people , and
priefts, Bishops, and paftors, and
vnder coulour of deceipt, feeke
to deceaue, and confound our
foules. So Iulian the Apoftate
vvith fire, and fvvord did perfecute religious men,and priefts,al-
though he did not put them to
death as S.Naz. faid,enuiēg thefe *Ora 1. in*
blefled faincts the crovvne of *Iuli.*
martirdome:yet he fpared no out
ragious crueltye,vvhich the malice of man could inuent to vex

trouble, and afflict these blessed
people, for so the oration of the
said Naz : vnto that apostate declared: vvherin he did offer himselfe a suter for all religious people (saieng) *si Philosophorum catum*
(sic enim eos appellat) qui nullo vin
culo humi teuentur, qui sola corpora
ac ne ea tota quidem possident ; qui
Cæsari nihil , Deo omnia debent
hymnos, preces , vigilias, lachrimas:
hos inquit si mitius tractaueris, &c.
If you deale gentlely (saith he)
vvith the schoole of Philosophers, for so he called thē, vvhich
vvere tied by noe earthlie obli-
gation vvhich did scarce possesse
their ovvne bodies, vvhich did
ovve nothing vnto Cæsar but all
vnto god, vnto vvhom they, by

their hymnes, prayers, vvatchinge, and tears vvere consecrated.
if you deale gentlely vvith the
seruants, and disciples of god,
vvhose daylie conuersation is in
heauen, vvho are the first fruite of
our lords flocke, the crovvnes of
faith, the precious margarits,
vvho are the stones of that temple, vvhose foundation, and corner stone is Christ, you shall do
vnto your self, and vnto vs a sin-
guler benefit this far S. Naz. In
all persecutions of the church
the pastors, and religious people
vvere first sett vppon: becaufe, as
it vvas saied, they barked against
those, that goe about to destroy
the flocke of Chrieft ; so the
prophet Hieremy saith, *formi-*

Thren. 47. do, & laqueus factus est nobis vati-
cinatio our prophesie doth pur-
chase nothing vntovs but the hal
ter, and occasion of trembling. so
vvere the prophets of the old lavv
afflicted, and put to cruell torments, amongest vvhome Mi-
cheas after being terribly bea-
ten, vvas cast into pryson, Vrias
vvas slayne, Hieremias after lōg
ymprisonment, terrible vvhip-
Ie.38,19.20 ping, and after cast into a dirtye
puddle of filth, vvherin he vvas
ovvervvhelmed, vvas stoned to
death; Isaias vvas cut in tvvaine
vvith a savv, and being sent by
god, they haue not omitted their
functions, notvvithstandinge all
the forces, and threatninges of
vvicked princes vvere bēt against

them : Sydrach, and Abednego *Daniel.3.1* *21.*
for refuſinge to adore the idole
of Nabuchodonoſor vvere caſt
into the burning fornace, and in
the midſt of the flames of ragin-
ge fire, they prayſed God. Daniel *Daniel 6.* *16.*
vvas caſt into the lyons den to be
deuoured.   Saul no ſooner fell
from God, then he put to death
50.prieſtes in Nobe, vvhy ſhould
then the prieſtes, and paſtors in
the lavve of grace meruaylé at *1 Reg 12* *18*
perſecutions, or feare the trou-
bles therof? do not they ſee their
head eleuated vppon the croſſe,
and nayled there vnto? vvas ther
not a Dragon before the vvoman vvhich vvas to be deliuered
of a childe, that no ſooner the
childe ſhould come into the

L   4

vvorld, but hee should bee deuou
red of the dragon, and this vvas
the caufe that Chrift faieth fpeaking to the perfecutors of the
church. *vos ex patre diabolo eftis, &*
defideria patris veftri vultis perficere
ille homicida fuit ab initio &c. you
are the children of the devill, &
ready to execute the vvil of your
father, for he vvas a murderer
from the beginning, vvhich euer
labored to deftroy Chrieft; fo the
deuil did vfe the helpe of Pharo
to kill all the fonnes of theHebre
ues, becaufe he thought that
Chrieft should defcend of that
natió accordinge to the flesh, but
Moyfes vvas deliuered, fignifienge
that Chrieft should efcape harme
leffe, he rayfed vp Aman to def-

troy all the said Hebreues, vvhich *Exe.7.*
he could not obtaine , he also
made an inftrument of Athalia *Reg.11.*
to blot out all the pofteritye of
Dauid, from vvhēce the Meffias
accordinge his humanitie vvas to
come into the vvorld , but Ioas
vvas deliuered: he ftirred vp alfo
Antiochus to taxe avvay and
confound the ftocke of Iacob *i.Ma. 2.*
laft of all vvhen the fulneffe of
time came in vvhichChrieft him
felf came:he vfed all pollicies by
Herodes cruelty toxill him:after-
vvardes hovv many follovvers of
Chrieft, and of his race vvere put
to death vnder *Nero* vnder *Noui-*
tiã, vnder *Traiã,* vnder *Adriã,* vn
der *Anthoni Verus, Seuerus, Ale-*
xander, by the furie of the people

L 5

vnder *Maximinus*, vnder *Decio*, *Va-*
leri⁹ Claudius Aurelianus, *Dioclesian⁹*
and *Maximianus* vnder *Iulian* in
the eaſt, in the vveaſt vnder *Valēs*
amongeſt the Goathes vnder *A-*
thanericus, vnder *Arcadius*, in Perſia
vnder *Ideger*, the *Vandal* perſecu-
tiõ vnder *Gēſericus* and *Hunericus*:
vvhat shal (I ſay? hovvmanyvvere
put to cruell death ſince that time, in all other countries, hovv
many bleſſed martirs did ſuffer by
the ſectes of Martine Luder and
bloudie Caluine, vvhich vvere ex-
citated, and ſtirred vp to deſtroy
Chrieſt, and the ſide of Abrahã,
vvhich is the catholicke church
and the ship of the apoſtles in
the mideſt of the ſea, and they
laboring in the ſame to ſaue

them selues, vvhich Chrieft did
behold, as venerable Beda faith *la* *Bed.hom's cap.2 8*
bor difcipuloru in remigando, & con-
trarius eis ventus, labores fanctæ Ec-
clefiæ varios defignat, quæ inter vn-
das feculi aduerfantis & immun-
dorum fpirituum flatus ad quietem
celeftë quafi ad fidam littoris ftatio-
nem peruenire conatur, the difficulties, that the apoftles had in bringing the ship to land, and the cõ
trarie vvindes they fuftained : do
declare the manifolde troubles
of the holie church: and being fo
fore afflicted, and grieuouflie
perfecuted, afvvel by the gentiles,
as by heretickes, it feemeth, if it
vvere poffible, that the redeemer
therof for a time vvould forfake
the fame: this much vener. Bed.

vvhat shall vvee fay of the fore
perfecutions of this age, vvhich
bringeth forth monftrous heretickes, fo many bloodie tirantes, fo
many falfe prophetes, of vvhom
Chrieft did fay, I haue not fent
them, and they did runne, I haue
not fpoken vnto them, and they
did prophefie, vvhich do vvatch
and laboure to corrupt, and defile our foules vvith their poifoned doctrine, vvhofe malitious
vvilles poifoned, and infected
vvith all kinde of hereticall impietie, and vvhofe vnderftanding
furnished vvith all deuilish pollicies and inuectiōsproceed novv fo
farre in their vvickednesse, and
hauing gotten fuch fucceffe in
their vvicked enterprifes, that

Kier.83.

if vvee had not fo firmlie, and fo ftedfaftlie builded vpon Chrieft his vvordes vvho promifed, that the gates of hell, should neuer preuaile againft his church, vvee should be afraid, that novv being inuironed vvith fo many enimies, being afflicted vvith fo many falfe prophetes, being tormented by fo many cruell bloodie tyrantes, being bought and folde by fo many impious polititiãs, and Machiuailes, being troubled by fo many apoftats: and forfaken of her bafe and rebellious children, it vvould novv be vtterlie deftroied.

❋❋❋❋❋❋❋❋❋❋❋

THE CHVRCH OF
god must suffer persecu-
tion, and thereby is ra-
ther reformed, then
destroyed.

CAP. IX.

IT is expedient, as-
vvell for the iustice
of god, as also for
the triall of the
good, that there
shouldebe heretikes, and vvicked
people, vvho shoulde bridle and
restraine our passions, and the furious inclination of our sensuali-

tie:for our corruption is such as
if by the discipline of vvicked
people(vvhich are as it vvere our
tutors)it vvere not repressed,vvee
vvould breake forth into such
madnesse,as the state of our saluation shoulde bee in danger:no
other vvise then a vvild horse
breakinge oftentimes the bridle
casteth of his rider.

By nature vve are the children
of vvrath , and the seruantes of
sinne, in vvhich vve be concea-
ued, and by vvhich vvee be corrupted and inclined to gape after
corruptible thinges.

This inclination vvas transfu-
sed,and brought from Adam vnto vs in our generation,and so in
vs it is naturall : and being depri-

ued of Original iuftice, in vvhich,
our firft parents vvere created:
(vvhich as the diuins do faye)vvas
the golden bridle to curbe the
flesh from rebellious infurrection
againft the fpirit, and the fame
beinge taken avvay, by the dolefull tranfgreffion of our faid pa-
rentes, vvithout any pofitiue
qualitie therunto adioyned,
man is carried avvay, and impelled by the nature of fenfuall appetits, vvhich is to follovve fen-
fualities and fenfible thinges oppofite and contrarie to the rule
of reafon:this Sainct Chry: cófide
ringe fayeth as a ship, that hath
loft her fterne,is toft too and fro,
not vvhether the pilot vvould,
but vvhere the tempeft driueth
                            her

her so man hauinge lost first this
golden sterne of original grace,
carried a vvay not vvhere reason
vvould direct, but vvhere vnrulie
appetits do mislead (this he said
of oure vnbridled luste, and dis-
position vnto base appetites) and
although this inclination in those that are baptised is not a sinne,
yet it prouoketh and disposeth
vs vnto sinne and is called by the
diuins) *fomes peccati*) vvhich is the
lavve of the flesh, vvhose desire
and affection is contrarie to the
desires of oure spirit: vvhich vvitnesseth S. Paul saieng I haue a *Rom. 6*
lavve in my members vvhich re-
sisteth the lavve of my minde, and
laboreth to make me vassall and
captiue to the lavve of sinne: and

M

and therfore he fayth, vvho shall
be able to deliuer me, from this
bodie of death: of vvhich cõplay-
neth holie Iob. faing *quare me feci-*
ſti contrarium tibi & factus ſum
mihi metipſi grauis : vvherfore haſt
thou framed me contrarie vnto
thee, and diſpleaſant vnto my ſelf:
and therfore he ſaid *non eſt auxi-*
lium mihi in me : and of my ſelf I
haue no healpe, by reaſon of his
inferiour parte diſpoſed to ſinne,
vvhich do perturbe and diuert vs
from the true path of the creator, and the rule of vertue, and
alſo maketh vvarre againſt the
ſuperior parte, vvhich is his ſpirit,
vvhich participatinge (as it vvere) vvith god, that rightlie amongeſt reaſonable creatures, ought

Iob 6.

to obtaine the place of gouerment, beinge by nature indued,
and enobled, vvith a beame of
heauenlie brightnesse, and to
bring them to any agreement, or
peaceable harmonie, the hand-
mayde must obey the mistresse,
and the bodie the soule, vvhich
cannot be brought to passe, but
by the force of extreame lavves,
that must be seuerlie executed
vpon a lavvlesse, and vnrulie seruant, vvhich S. Paul extended ri-
gourously tovvarde his ovvne bo
die saieng *castigo corpus meum &*
in seruitutem spiritus redigo carnem
meam, *&c.* I chastice my bodie
and reduce my flesh vnto the ser-
uitude of the spirit: the like all the
sanictes haue don, by fasting, vva-

1. Cor. 9

M 2

chinge prayēg, and other austere
vvorkes of religion, and pennāce,
and by this meās haue gotten the
vpper hād of this slaue, and rebellious seruant, not onlie reuolteth
from the spirit, but also dravveth
the spirit from god , by reason of
vvhose rebellion, vvee be come
disloyall vnto his commandementes, insensible to his inspira-
tions , vnthankefull vnto his benefites, careles of his diuine iustice, obliuious of his mercie , and
forgetfull of our ovvne saluation, and god almightie, for a iust
punishment vvhich vvee haue
deserued, permitteth, for that our
soule vvould not obey god,
shoulde become a slaue vnto the
fleshe, vvhich is his ovvne slaue

vvhich S. Auguſt. doth verifie
quoniam anima ſuperiorem dominum
ſuo arbitrio deſeruerat inferiorem
famulum (carnem) ad ſuum arbitriū
non tenebat. becauſe the ſoule, by
the libertie of free vvill, did forſake god oure ſupreme lorde, the
inferiour vvhich is the fleſh ren-
dreth not that obedience vnto
the ſoule accordin ge vnto the
ſlauerie of the one, and libertie of
the other, not that the ſoule
hath no povver to command, and
conſtraine the fleſhe to obey, for
it hath free vvil to do and vndo
vvhat liketh it beſt, andas S. Aug.
ſaith *voluntate propria quiſque ma-*
lus & none committeth ſinne
but by his freevvill and ſo he ſaid
ream linguam non facit niſi rea mens

Deciuitate
Dei lib. 1 ʒ
c. 14

Aug. de
ui. lib. 1. ci
1 ꝉ.

our toung is not guiltie, but by
our guiltie minde, vvhich he con

Aug. deci l.
13 c.14
Aug. lib. 14
cap. 13

firmed in his 14. booke *nec care*
corruptibilis animam peccatricem:
sed anima peccatrix fecit esse corru-
ptibilem carnem nether the corruptible flesh maks a sinnefull soule,
but the sinnefull soule makes the
flesh corruptible, for the greatest,
difficultie, that vve haue to
supprise the flesh, & the vnre aso-
nable concupiscence therof pro-
cedes of the longe custome, and
continuance of the soule in sinne
as the said S. Aug. saith *libidini*
dum seruitur facta est consuetudo, &
dum consuetudini non resistitur, fa-
cta est necessitas. our luste beinge
obeyd is be come a custome, and
this custome beinge not qui-

quicklie reſtrained grovveth vnto
an neceſſitie of nature vvhich can
be hardlie repelled, and ſo Ariſt
ſaith *voluntas adhærens peruerſo fi-*
ni non poteſt diu carere praua ele-
ctione. our vvill tending vnto an
ill end vnto vvhich it is impelled
and moued by this ſaid bad inclination cannot be longe vvithout
bad means to put it in execution:
for the outvvard obiectes, and
occaſions by vvhich it is moued,
as alſo the internall paſſions of
our baſe affection by vvhich it is
daylie ſollicited,& ouerruled, do
ſo peruert our iugement , blinde
our vnderſtanding , infect our
vvilles,as vve may ſay vvith the
prophet *defecit me virtus mea &*
lumen oculorum meorum non eſt me-

D. Aug.
Ariſt.lii

M 4

cum my force did faile me and I
haue not the vse of my sight: this
he said by reason of his great fall
fromgods grace of vvhich beinge
depriued he vvas blinded vvith
brutish cōcupiscence and made a
slaue vnto his passions therfore
he said *possederunt nos alij domini
absque te*: vve forsake the o god
and do yeeld our selues to other
lordes vvhich are our sinister desires vvhich vvee follovve, and
self vvill vvhose vnresonable
commandementes vvee obey, the
vvhichhath so grieuouslie vvounded our soules that it can neuer
be cured, but at the great coste
and charges of our said proper
vvill that inflicted the same, and
as svvelling vlcersmust be healed

be hoat burning iron, by vvhich
the deadlie canker vvich lieth
vnder the flesh may be taken
avvay, fo this poyfoned canker
vvhich lurketh in our heartes
and gnavveth our intrailes, by
vvhich vvee languish and pine
avvay, cannot be healed but by
sharpe medicine of troubles and
perfecutions, and as the apoftle
faith *virtus in infirmitate perficitur*   2.Cor.i2
the perfection of vertu is made
knovven in aduerfitie, for as Ro-
fes the more they be preft the
better they fmel, frankencenfe
before it be caft vnto the fire shevveth not his vertue, nor our fleshe before it be feuerlie punished, and reftrained of her per-
nicious, & dangerous libertie ac-

M   5

knovvledged eyther superiour, to
command it, or lavve to bridle
and direct it: Alexander the great
beinge vvounded vvith an arro-
vve in his side, did acknovvledge
him self to be a mortal mã, vvhere
as before through victories gottē in so many battailes, & the cõ
quest obtained ouer so many nations, vvas so proude, that he cõ-
manded him self to be adored as
god, therfore the holie ghost
Prouer. 28. said _beatus est homo qui semper est_
pauidus. Happie is that man that
is alvvaies fearful of him self. by
libertie vve become dissolute, and
carelesse, by restraint vvareful, &
circumspect, the Romans giuinge
libertie vnto the Bactrians for
that they did succour the Con-

ſul Rufus in the ſpartan vvarres,
they refuſed it, ſaynge that by libertie they should become ſlaues. The common vvealth of the
Lacedemoniãs being ſo glorious,
& renovvmed in many excellent
vertues, ſo ſoone at it began to liue at quiet, preſentlie declined,
and at length fell to ruine, the
vvhich may be Knovven and
verified of the Romans, by the
contention that vvas betvvixt
Cato and Scipio Naſica : Cato
vvas of opinion that Carthage
should be altogither deſtroid.
Scipio vvould haue it preſerued,
for that the Romans hauing no
aduerſaries abroade through
longe peace, and quietneſſe,
should be vveakned: vvoe be vn-

ro you Rome, saith he, if Carthage
stande not; for external vvarres
being ended, then intestine va-
riance, and ciuill discorde vvas re-
nevved betvvixt the Romains
them selues, vvhich vvas the cause of greater calamitie amonge
them, then all the forraine vvarres they had against their forai-
ne enimies.

The vniuersal peace of the
church vvas the cause, that manye horrible dissentions, and dangerous schismes vvere amongest
church mē, amōge vvhō through
long quietnesse, the key of knovv
ledge fayled in many, iniquitie did
abound, and charitie vvaxed colde vverfore Isaiah, cried out *in*

pace amaritudo mea amarissima

in peace I am moſt diſquieted,
and as S. Auguſtine ſaith the per
ſecution of tirantes is grieuous,
the perſecution of hereticxes is
vvorſe, but that of voluptuous
pleaſures and quiet reſt, is the
moſt dangerous of all; becauſe as
S. Chryſoſt. ſaide *tormenta facie-* *D.Chryſ.*
bant martyres: blandimenta vero
Epicuros. torments makes martyrs,
pleaſures epicures, of vvhich peace the ſpouſe in the canticles
(ſaith) *nigra ſum ſed formoſa filie* *Cant.1.v.ð*
Hieruſalem. I am blacke but
vvell fauored (o daughters of
Hieruſalem) vvhich vvordes
Origenes interpreted to be
ſpoken of the ſoule of man,
vvhich by the grace gotten
in affliction , is purified,

and made beautifull, vvhich before by longe quietnes, and our
corruptible inclination t e iūto,
vvas deformed. Dauid through
long peace, and tranquilitie of
spirituall consolation, said, *in abū-*

Psal.29. *dantia mea non mouebor in æternum*
in abundance of long rest, and di-
uine consolation I shal neuer be
moued; vvhich vvas the cause as
S. Basil saith that Dauid fell so
grieuouslie, and said after vvardes
non est pax ossibus meis my bones

Psal.37. haue no rest, *& in flagellis paratus*
sum:& dolor meus in conspectu meo
semper?:I prepare my self for gods
discipline, and my grief is alvvaies
before myne eyes, and left the
manifold graces, and priuiledges
of the apostle should bethe occa-

fion of his fall of he should take
pride therof or thinke him self fe-
cure,and void of any danger, he
faid *ne magnitudo reuelationum ex-* 2.*Corin.*11
tollat me , &*c.* leaft the manifold
reuelations of god should puffe
me vp, the ftinge of the flesh
vvhich is the angell of Satan
doth buffet me;it vvas faid vnto
Adam by god *maledicta terra in* *Gene.3.*
opere tuo:in laboribus comedes de ea,
fpinas & *tribulos, germinabit tibi*
curfed is the earth in thy vvorke
in thy labour thou shalt eat thy
bread , thorns and thistles it shal
bring forth vnto thee , and al-
tlough there vvere no deuill to
tempt vs, the flesh that bringeth
forth the faid briers , ad thistles
tempteth vs, and endeuoreth to

defile vs,vvith her raging concu
piscence , the vvorld laboreth
vvith his vanitie to ouerthrovv
vs,the soule vvith her pride to
confound vs,and besides there is
a deuil that vexeth vs,and tepteth
vs to fall avvay fro god euery day

ad Eps.6 .   *quia hic enim nobis colluctatio aduersus carnem & sanguinem sed ad-
uersus principes , &c.* For vvee do
not onlie sttuggle vvith flesh, and
blood:bnt vvee haue our combate against the povver,and strength
of the princes of darknesse, as
longe as vvee liue, in this vvorld
vvee ought not to expect peace,
and as longe as vvee be copassed
vvith so many aduersaries vvee
ought not to feare their inuasios,
and as longe as vvee are sailinge

in

in the dangerous sea of thisvvorlde in vvhich vvee muſt paſſe
throughe the dangerous gulfe of
death vve muſt paſſe by the narrovue vvay of pennance, and
mortification, if vvee meane to
come vnto life, and not through
the broad vvide vvay of pleaſures, vnles vvee intende to fall into confuſion. ther is nothinge ſo
hurtefull for a chriſtian ſoldiour,
as the pleaſures of this vvorld,
vnto vvhich vvee dedicat our ſelues if vvee had no aduerſaries to
vvithdravv vs from them. the ſoldiours of Hanniball after the famous victorie obtained in the
battle of Canas againſt the Romans, through vvanton pleaſures
and reſt, vnto vvhich they gaue

N

them selues, at Capua vvere after
so softened, and enfeebled, that
they, vvhich vvere able to indure great traueles, and sustaine
much labour vvherby they did
vvinne many battles, against the
Romans, vvere by their ovvne
quietnes, and pleasures, vanqui-
shed, and ouercome by their said
enimies: all ecclesiasticall histo-
ries do beare vvitnesse that the
church of Christ, is subiect to
confusion, and danger in time of
any peace, or quietnesse: S. Ci-
prian also doth verifie the same:
Dominus inquit probare suam fami-
liam voluit, & quia traditam nobis
diuinitus disciplinam, pax longa cor-
ruperat iacentem fidem & pæne di-
xerim dormientem censura cœlestis

Plut. in vi-
ta Hamb.

Cyp. serm.
de lapsis.

erexit · studebant singuli augendo patrimonio, non in sacerdotio religio deuota, non in præsbiteris fides integra, non in operibus misericordia, non in moribus disciplina: our lord, saith he, vvould trie his familie, and be cause gods religion vvas corrupted by longe peace, and our faith vvhich languished, by long quietnesse, vvas by celestiall correction raised vp: euerie one did studie hovv to augment his patrimonie: in preisthood no deuotiõ vvas obserued: in churchmen faith vvas not sincerlie kept: their vvorkes vvere vvithout mercie: and their manners vvithout discipline; this infamie, and disorder brought in by the tranquilitie of the church, as the good martyr

D. Aug. de vera relig. c. 8.

telleth, vvas reformed, by the persecution and troubles therof, for
as, S. Aug. saith *multa ad fidem ca-*
tholicam pertinentia dum heretico-
rum callida inquietudine vexantur:
the vexations, and disquietnesse
of heretickes redovvndeth to the
good of the catholick faith, that
it may re defended against them,
that it may be more dulie exami-
ned more diligentie considered,
more ductifullie obserued, more
clearlie vnderstode, more feruen-
tlie preached, and being brought
in question by the aduersarie,
may be religiouslie embraced, so
god may be glorified, Chriest honored, our fayth renovvmed, the
constancie of the good confirmed, the vveake strengthned, the

hereticke confounded and Sa-
than ouerthrovven thus farre S.
Aug. vnto vvhich agreeth Sainct
Chryf. *virtus fidei in periculis secu-*
ra est, in securitate periclitatur the
vertue of faith in danger, is secu-
re, in securitie is in danger, for nothing faith he abateth the force
o fayth, somoch as long peace,
holie Arsenius, after that he obtained of god to be deliuered of
some temptations, by vvhich he
vvas attached, and finding him
felf by long reft, and quietneffe to
be more negligent, and careles of
him felf, did reneue his combat
vvith him felf, and fought of god
the former temptations, this vvas
the caufe that god gaue leaue to
the deuill to vex Iob , gods mea-

Chry. in
Math. 20.

N 3

ning vvas nothing els, then to e-
xercife his vertue, vvhich becō-
meth mortified vvith trauels,
and contradiction : the vvheat
that is not turned, is eaten vvith
vvefels, the garment that is not
vvorne: is eaten vvith mothes, the
timber that is not feafoned : is
fpoiled vvith coftlickes, the iron
that is not vvrought, is confu-
med vvith ruft, bread long kept
grovveth mouldie, the fayth of
euerie chriftian is the better if it
be tried, the goodneffe of euerie
thinge is knovven by the exercife
therof, and fo your fayth shalbe
novve perceaued by your temptation and perfecution, vvhich is
the fire according to S. Auguftin:
quo aurum rutilat, palia confumitur,

perficitur peccator ne misere pereat,
by vvhich the gold is tried, the
rust is consumed, the sinner purified, and made perfect, that he
should not perish miserablie, vnto vvhich agreed. S. Iohn Chryf.
Vt infirmatur peccator aduersis : sic
iustus tentationibus roboratur, as
the sinner is vveakened by aduersitie: so the iust is confirmed therby: although many of you in this
persecution shal denie Chrieft,
yet I hope Chrieft shalbe more
glorified by such as shall confeffe
him vnto their death, then his
church scādalized, by such as shal
forsake the same : affuring your
selues, that there is no other cause
vvhy god doth suffer this perfecution againft his church, thē for

Chryf.lib.4
serm. 1. de
martyro-
log. cam. 3.

N 4

the good of you, that are the mēbers therof, and for the exercise,
and practise of your vertue, and
manifold influences of godes grace bestovved vppō you by vvhich
you may be defended against your
aduersaries. God did suffer amongest the childrē of Israel Iebeseus
to exercise ther strength, and to
trie their vallure: god did assure
them the land of promise, but no
ne did inter vnto it, but such as
ouercame the fierse inhabitātes
therof, against vvhom the Israeli-
tes vvere to fight; no more can
vvee inter into the promised lande of heauen, vnles vve ouercome
couragiouslie the deuiles, and
his instrumentes, vvhich indevvo-
red to hinder vs of the passage

therof, for vvhich they so often
prouoke vs to the skirmish, and
therfore god permitteth heretickes for the triall of catholickes,
the vvicked for the exercise of the
good, and varres againſt his sol-
dieurs to giue them a glorious
crovvne if they vvil ouercome, a
paye for ther paine, a revvard for
ther laboure, and glorie if they
vvill fight valiantlie.

THE BLOOD OF
*Martyrs is the seed of the
church which more increa-
seth by the suffrance of godlie
people.*

CAP. X.

He naturall histo-
ries do declare,
that ther is no bet
ter remedie for
a withered tree, to
bring fourth fruite:
then to sprinckle , and moysten
the bodie therof vvith the blood
of man: so the church of god

vvhich did feeme to vvither a-
vvay, and decay by longe peace
and reſt vvith the bloode of martyrs doth floriſh vvith ſainctes,
and holie men. according to Ter-
tulian: *ſanguis martyrum eſt ſemen*
chriſtianorum: & granum cadens in
terram vbi mortuum fuerit multum
fructum affert, the bloode of martyrs is the ſeede of chriſtians, and
the graine that falleth vnto the
earth vvhen it is dead, bringeth
fourth abundance of fruict, the
bleſſed Ignatius ſaid that he him
ſelf vvas one of the grains of
Chrieſt: for if the graine be not
dead in the earth, there grovveth
no fruite of it, if Chrieſt had not
died for the church, none had
bin a martyr, and becauſe he ſuffe

Tert.in
Ap.1o.12

red for his church being his spouse, she indeauoreth to revvard
him in the same coyne, and to giue vnto him blood for blood, and
Exo. 4. & so she saies in Exodus and in the
Psal. 115. Psal. *quid retribuam Domino pro*
omnibus quæ retribuit mihi · vvhat
shall I render vnto him for all
that he geueth vnto me : *qui dile-*
Apo. 1. *xit nos & lauit nos a peccatis nostris*
sanguine suo: vvhich loued vs and
vvashed vs from our sinnes : the
church doth both promisse, and
performe saieng *calicem salutaris*
Psal. 115. *accipiā, & nomen Domini inuocabo.*
Math 5. 26
I vvill pleadge him in that bitter
challice, vvhich he druncke vnto
vs. he vvas the first, that druncke
of this cup, and the first graine of
his gospell that vvas dead in the

èarth, and *primogenitus mortuorum*
the firft child that intred the celeftiall paradice, and therfore many bleffed children are alfo dead
vvith him, by vvhofe fufferance
and death god is glorified, the
church honored, fuftained, and e-
ftablished, as a certaine holie martyr faith *Sanguine fundata eft Eccle-
fia, fanguine cæpit. Sanguine fuccreuit
fanguine finis erit.* by bloode the
church vvas funded, by bloode it
began, by blood it continued, and
by blood shall haue an end. as
a man caunot liue but, by the
death, and blood of many beaftes vvhich are ordained for his
fuftentation, fo the church
of Chrieft, cannot vvell
be fuftayned, but by the

the blood of holie martyrs.   In
the old synagoge, vvilde beaftes
vvere offered vnto god in facrifice, by vvhich god vvas conten-
ted, but novve in the lavve of
grace, not onlie the blood of
Chrieft, vvas abondantlie offered
vnto him. but alfo the blood of
infinite bleffed martyrs, as the pro
phet faith: *effuderant fanguinem fan*
Etorum tuorum ficut aquam in circui
tu Hierufalem. they haue fhed the
blood of thy faindes, as if it vvere
vvater in the circuit of Hierufalem, *qui fanguinem fanEtorum &*
prophetarum effuderunt: vvhich did
shed the blood of the faindes,
& of the prophetes, for there are
offered more men vnto god in facrifice in the lavve of grace, then

Pfal. 78.

Apoca. 16.

vvere beaftes in the olde lavv:and
as S.Hierom.vvirnesseth for euerie day in the yeere fiue thovvfand martyres vnto his age : and
fince hovv many thovvfand did
fuffer?although the tyrantes did
indeauoure to rafe the regifters
of bleffed martyrs:yet vve finde,
by fuch as be extant,that his com
putation is true , though it be rather vvonderfull then incredible;
for at one time 200. 300. 400.
600.togither vvas nothinge, and
that dailie,and oftentimes,2000.
3000.and more,fome times in at
fricke 4966. vnder Hunericus
king of the Goathes , amongeft
vvhome there vvere manye bishops, prieftes, deacons, and lay
people vvhich did receaue the

Epift.ad shron & Heliodo,

Martyro log 12. O- ctob.

crovvne of martyrdome. I make
no mention of the 6000. that
vvere all put to death vvith their
captaine Mauritius, nor of the
1000. that vvere crucified by
Adrian, and Antonie imperors in
the montaine Ararar, nor of the
100001. Virgins that vvere put
to death by the Hunns. but I cannot keepe silēce, that a vvhole citie in phrigia vvas destroied by
the persecutor: so as neyther vvoman nor childe did escape the furie of the slaghter, such vvas the
rage of the infernal dragon, vvho
laboreth to ouerflovve the earth
vvith the bloode of martyrs,

Apud
Græcos 26
decem.

In the Calender of February
28. in the citie of Nicomedia by
the commaundement of Maximinus

minus 200. chriftians vvere brent
in the 2. of Februarie in the fame
Calender 3000. vvhich did fuffer
at Rome and 3000. that did fuffer
at Hierufalem by Cofdore, vvhat
shal I fpeake of all the dayes of
the yeare of all other countries,
and places : the number that ended their liues by extreame tormentes, none knovveth, but he,
that predeftinated them, and hath
giuen them grace to fuffer, as alfo a crovvne for their fufferance,
fo as the church may fay vnto
Chrieft that, vvhich the vvife of
Moyfes faid vnto him at the cir-
cumcition of his fonne *fponfus fã-* Exod.4.
guinis tu mihi es you are vnto me
the fpoufe of bloode, euen as the
feed, that is fovven in the fielde

O

bringeth foarth no fruit, but by
raine, and heat of the sunne: so
the catholicke religion, vvhich is
the seede, that is sovven in his
church bringeth neyther holi-
nesse or pietie vvith it, vnles it
be vvatered by the blood of
Chriest,&his martirs,neyther cã,
it bud fourth,but by the burning
and inflaming heat of the holie
gost vvhich isthe fire that Chriest
did saye should burne in the hear
tes of his blessed martyrs:vvhich
are like as S.Augustine sayth vnto
the childrẽ of Israel in Aegipt the
more they vvere oppressed, the
more they did multiplie: and as

Leo Papa
in serm.de
natali alo-
rũ Pet. &
Pauli.

Leo Papa saieth : *Ecclesia non mi-*
nuitur persecutionibus , sed augetur,
& semper Dominicus ager segete di-

tiore vestitur, dum grana quæ singu-la cadent multiplicata nascuntur, nam occiso vno martyre plures sur-gebant fideles. The church by per-secution diminisheth not, but ra-ther increaseth, and our lordes feilde is the more richer, that ma-ny graines do fall in it, becausе that euerie one doth multiplie, for one martyr beinge made, many christians do rise and S. Am-brose saith *sicut vinea dum ligatur erigitur & rescissa non minuitur sed augetur ita sancta plebs*, &c. as the vine being tied riseth vp, being lopped and cut, it increaseth: so the people of god vvhen they be humbled, they be promóted vnto vvhich agreeth Cassiodorus. *nouit Ecclesia beneficia Domini: triumpha-*

Amb.lib.9 c.10.su lu-cam.

lib.variar.u

O 2

*re de suis cladibus, ingrauata persecu-
tionibus si quidem proficit, afflictione
semper augetur, sanguine martyrum
irrigatur, tristitia magis erigitur, an-
gustia dilatatur, fletibus pascitur, ie-
iunijs reficitur: deinde potius crescit
vnde mundus deficit.* The church
knovveth godes benefites, to
triumph for her calamities: for
being loden vvith persecution
she profiteth, by afflictiõ alvvayse
increaseth, vvith the blood of
martyrs she isvvatered, vvith hea-
uinesse she is exalted, vvith
streightnesse she is enlarged, vvith
teares she is nourished, vvith fasting it is refressed, and in one
vvord it prospereth vvith that by
vvhich the vvorld decaieth :and
therfore S. Augustine saieth, that

although by the perſecution of
heretickes, the church doth ſuffer many tribulations, yet Chrieſt
turneth all that perſecutió to the
good of his ſeruantes, vvhich by
their tribulation, and affliction do
obtaine thoſe bleſſinges, vvhich *Math. 5.*
Chrieſt in his goſpell promiſeth:
ſaieng bleſſed be you vvhen you
ſhalbe perſecuted, for this perſecution, and for his death ended
therin, the bleſſed martyr ſainct
Cypriã gaue god thankes vvhen
the ſentence of death vvas pro-
nounced againſt him.

O 3

OF GODS PV-
nishmentes which he infli-
cteth vpon persecutors, al-
though for a time they florish.

GAP. XI.

Abac. 1.
Psal. 72.
Hier. 12
Iob 21

I *Vstus es Domine* saith Hiere. *& iusta loquar ad te, quare via impiorum prosperatur, &c.* Thou art iust (o lorde) and iustlie I vvill aske of thee, vvherfore do the vvicked prosper? here the holie man vvould faine put vp a bill

of complaint againit god for suffering vvicκed, and tranfgreffors
of his lavve to profper. S. Auguftine anfvvereth to this queftion
faieng *Deus cuius bonitas eft poten-*
tia, &c. god vvhofe goodneffe is
his might and being omnipotent
good, out of the euill he vvrea-
fteth good in difpofing, and con-
uertting the euill vnto goodneffe,
& by the payne, and punifhmen-
te of finne, repaireth and amen-
deth the badneffe of finne, for if
euill vvere not, there fhoulde be
no vfe of vindicatiue iuftice to
punifh it, or of patience to be e-
xercifed by it and fo he faieth, *me-*
lius enim Deus iudicauit de malis
benefacere, quam mala nulla effe per-
mittere: it is more conuenient to

O 4

Aug. Ench
c.11 & de
ordi.nec. y
laft. lib. de
ira Dei. yfi-
dor. lit de
fummo bo-
no Eufeb de
præpa Euā
gelica lib 3
Aug lib de
ciuii c 8 &
lib 13 c 28

aug Euch c
25 26 tom
3

224   *A Mnemosynum to the*
gods iugement to conuert the e-
uill vnto good , then to suffre no
ne at all, & therfore he said that
euill, and vvicked people are suf-
aug in Pſ
54 v I fered, that god his vvonderfull
goodneſſe may be knovven, *omnis*
malus aut ideo viuit, vt corrigatur,
aui ideo viuit, vt per illum bonus exer
ceatur and ſo euils are ſuffered,
eyther for their correction , that
do committ them , or for their
triall, that do ſuffer them. for as in
man there is no goodneſſe vvithout patience, vvhich euill vvorkes: ſo there is no euill vvithout
paine vvhich follovveth ſinne as
the shadovv the bodie according
Rom a to S. Gregorie ; vnto vvhich a-
greeth the apoſtle, *ira & indigna-*
tio, &c. anger, vvrath tribulation,

and anguish vppon the foule,
that vvorketh iniquitie:vvherup-
pon S.Aug.faith *voluifti Domine,*
*&c.*it is thy vvill, o lord , and fo
vvee knovve it by experience,
that a difordered foule is a fufficient punifhment for it felf. Hier.
verifieth this alfo *fcito & vide,*
knovv and beholde,vvhat a dolefull thing it is,to forfake god, and
not to be poffeffedvvith his feare.

Aug.lib. 2.
conf.c.12

Hier. 2.

God maketh a vvhip of the
vvicked to punifh the faultes,and
reforme the liues of his children,
and as the father cafteth the rodd
into the fire,vvith vvhich he corrected his children : fo god dealeth vvith thefe vvicked people,
vvhom he permitteth to increafe
in their mifchief,&vvicked plotts

O 5

vntill such as be predestinated be
corrected, gods vvrath appeased,
and the reprobate be brought to
their vtter confusion, and so cast
into that endles fire ordained for
them: *qui nocet, noceat adhuc: & qui*
in sordibus est sordescat: he that hur-
teth, let him hurte as yet, and he
that is defiled: let him be defiled
as yet. that god suffers the vvicked to go on in their vvicked pur
poses, and to afflict the good, his
principall intention is the refor-
mation, & saluatiō of the one, &
not the damnation of the other:
but vvoe be vnto the vvicked
that are ordained to reforme the
vices of others, vvhen they them
selues are rather deformed then
reformed: the like vvoe vvas pro-

Apoc. 22.

Isa. 10.

nounced againſt Aſſur, and yet by
Iſaias he vvas called the rod of
gods furie, and the club of his anger and yet by the ſaid prophet it *Iſa. 31.*
is ſaid Aſſur ſhall fall by the ſvvo-
erd, and his children ſhalbe ſlaues ; god did raiſe vp Saule as S.
Cyprian ſaies to afflict the peo- *Cyp. lib. 3*
ple of Iſrael vvith manifold im- *b. p. 9.*
poſitions, and exactions for contemning Samuell, or rather god
in him: after vvardes the ſaid Saul
forgetting him ſelf, and deſpiſing
the ſaid Samuel, vvas depoſed of
his kingdome , and depriued of
his life, god ſuffred Achab to per-
ſecute the Prophet Mycheas,
but Achab vvas ſlaine after vvardes of his enimies ; Iorā the ſonne
of Achab, and all his progenie

vvere put to death by Iehu; I vvill
said the prophet vnto Iehu requi
re the blood of all the seruantes
and Prophetes of god at the handes of Iesabell. Vvhen Zacharias
the prophet vvas murdered in the
house of god, at his death he said
Videat Dominus & requirat : let
god beholde and reuenge, the seruantes of King Ioas, by vvhose
vvill he dyed, insulted vppon the
said Ioas, and slue him in his bed.
Amasias King of Iuda, for the like
offence had no better ende, his
sonne Ozias for vsurping the function of the priest, vvas strocken
vvith a leprosie: vvho vvould not
feare asvvell the horrible punishmentes of the rebellious conuen-
ticle of Chore Dathã, and Abi-

4 Reg. 3i.

3. Reg. 3i.

3 Reg 22

4 Reg 9

2 para 14
2 para 29

rā, vvho for not obeing Moyſes,
and Aaron vvere ſvvallovved *Ezech 5*
of the earth; as alſo that of Ma-
naſſes the perſecutor of Iſaias,
and Zedechias the perſecutor of *Zach 2 4*
Hieremie *qui vos tāgit &c.*vvhich
toucheth you ſaieth the holie
ghoſt toucheth the apple of mine
eie.Chrieſt ſaith the blood of Za- *Luc 11*
charias the prophet, vvhom you
haue killed betvvixt the temple,
and the alter, ſhalbe required at
your handes.the moſt grieuouſe
calamities, and horrible puniſh-
mentes of the vagabōd diſperſed
ievves throughout all natiōs, their
hardeneſſe of heart, and obduration in their infidelitie, vnto
vvhich their vvilfull, and blinde
paſſions haue brought them,their

incorrigible, and vntractable humoures, vvhich by no reason, or
auctoritie of scripture can be reclaymed, is nothing els then gods
iust iudgment executed vppon
them by the Romans, (to auoid
vvhose gouerment they put
Chriest to death)for the blood of
our sauiour, according to their
ovvne decree:*sanguis eius super nos
&c.*saieng:let is blood light vpon
vs,and our posteritie. Pilat then
president of iurie that gaue sentē-
ce of death against him and condemned him,vvas partaker of the
pnnishmentes inflicted for the
same(as Eusebius and Nycepho-
rus do vvrite)for being in disgra-
ce byTyberius the emperour,and
banished by Caius and being tor-

Euse.Hyst.
Eccl.lib.2.
c.7. Nycep
lib.2. c.10.

mented by his guiltie confcience,
did kill him felf. vnto the like miferable ende, Anna, and Cayphas
vvere fubiect as thofe authours
do vvright. It is recorded by all
ecclefiafticall hiftories that perfecutors do feldome efcape a bad
ende, omitting pagan princes, I
thought good to fet dovvne a fe-
vve exãples of hereticall tyrãntes
and of fome catholickes. Conftã-
tius the Arrian emperour, and a
greaet perfecutor of Liberius rhe
Pope, & of S. Athanafius & other
catholicke bishops vfurping vnto
him felue the determinatiõ of ec
clefiafticall caufes, ended moft
miferablie as the faid Ath. vvit-
neffeth, Valés, a cruell perfecutor
of the church and of Ifai the mõ-

Atha. epi.
ad foluta-
riam vni-
agenics

Amianus
Marcell.
lib. 22.
Ambr. lib.
3:

cke for reprouing him for his
crueltie, vvas by the Goathes
vvith many of his nobilitie bur-
ned in flieng from them.

Valentinian the yonger a great
perfecutor of S. Ambrofe vvas
hanged by his ovvne feruantes as

*amb lib 5
epiſtolaris
3 2*

the faid S. Ambro.declareth.Ana
ſtaſius a great perfecutor of prieſtes,and religious people,& therfore excomunicated by Gelaſius

*Eutrop 4
op 34*

the Pope vvas ſtrocken dovvne
by a thunderbolte as Eutropius
vvriteth.Mauritius the emperoure a great diſturber of S.Gregorie,
vvho thus vvritt vnto him , if the
ſinnes of Gregorie faied he be
ſuch, as they be infufferable, the
ſinnes of S. Peter are not ſuch,
vvhofe place I holde, vvas apprehended,

hended by an ordinarie souldier
of his ovvne called Phoca, hauing exalted him self vnto the
emperiall throne, after killing
his vvife, and children in his presence, did hang him self vppon a
gibber, and being vppon the lad-
der, he vttered these vvordes
iustus es Domine, &c. O lord thou
arte iust, & right is thy iudgmēt,
Constance the nephevv of Hera-
clius, vvhich banished Martine
the Pope, vvas slayne in Cicilia of
his ovvne seruantes: the like end
did happen also vnto Michael the
emperour. vvhat should I remember the death of Constantius the
sonne of Leo, of Henry the 4. the
first emperour of the vveast, of
Frederick the 2. Frederk Barba-

Blundus li 3 decad 1 I aulnsdea covus li 18

Sen ann to 3 in Consti ce & Me-chaele

P

234   *A Mnemosynum to the*

Sigeber ad ann 778 rosa, Philip, Otho the 4. Cōradus, Manfredus Lodouick the 4. and other emperours, and kinges that vvere great persecutors of the church, and of the pastors therof as Nauclerus, Genebrard, Cæsar Baro. do vvitnes, vvhich also do declare the miserable end of many kinges, and princes of England. for expelling and banishing bishops out of their seuerall dioces Beda lib 4 cap 26 hist Ecclef also the said Cæsar Baro. anno, Domini 684. and venerable Beda do testifie the miserable end of Efridus king of the North parte of Englãd. I vvill put dovvne the said Beda his ovvne vvordes translated out of Latin; Elfridus hauĩg sent Bertus vvith an armie into Ireland, vvasted and spoiled most

miserablie the innocēt nation &
alvvaies most freindlie vnto the
english, so as the svvorde of the
enimie did not spare church, or
monasterie, the people of the I-
land resisted them the best they
could, and called, on gods helpe
against them & to reuenge their
affliction, and although cursers,
and ill tongued cannot possesse
the Kingdom of heauen, yet it is
beleued, such as vvere cursed for
their impietie, did the sooner receaue punishment, according
their deserte god exacting the fame, vvheras the yeere follovving
the said King rashlie, and vvithout aduise of his councell, and
against the vvill of Cutbert of
blessed Memorie, vvhich vvas of

P 2

late made bishop , inuaded his
neighbours dominions, and being
brought vnto great streightnes
and difficultie, his armie, and him
self vvas slayne the yeere of his
adge 40. and of his raigne the 15.
& his freindes did prohibite him
to enterprise this vvarre, but be
cause the yeere before he refused
to heare the most reuerend father Egebert, that he should not
impugne and afflict Ireland hur-
ting him nothing, it is giuen him
as a pnnishment not to heare
those that laboured to vvithdravve him from destructiõ, from
vvhich time the povver of England began to ebb, and decline
this farre venerable Beda a holie
sainct of the english nation if

Oza for touchinge the Arcke of
god being a place vvheare the table of the lavve, Moyses rodd and
other relickes vvere kept, vvas ² *Reg* 7
ftrocken dovvn dead vvith a thū-
derbolt. the beaftes vveare ftoned
to death for going vppon the
montaine. vvhy should not reafo
nable people be feuerlie puni- 4 *Reg* 13
shed of god for embrevving their
murdering handes vvith the in-
nocent blood of his faintes,
vvhich be not dead thinges, as the
arck vveare, but the liuing rēples
of the holie ghoaft, vvhich are
mediators betvvixt god, and mā:
vvhofe auctoritie geuen vnto thē
by Chrieft exceedeth the povver
and iurifdiction eyther of kinges
vpon the earth, or angels in hea-

P   3

uen vvhich haue povver ouer
the soules of monarkes, and em-

Io 10 Mat
2 18
perours, vnto vvhom our sauiour
sayth vvhose sinnes soeuer you
forgiue in earth they shalbe for-
giuen in heauen, &c. of vvhom,

Pet c 2
S. Peter saith *Vos autem genus ele-*
ctum, regale sacerdotium gens sancta
&c. you are the chosen stocke,
the hinglie priesthoode, theh olie
familie, people pickt out, that you
should declare his vvonders &c.
although many priestes be ignorant, and full of imperfections, for
amongest so many, there must be
som good & some bad the church
of Christ being like vnto rhe net
of the gospell , that dravverh all
sort of fishes. for in this church
vvee say *dimitte nobis* , &c. forgi-

uevs onr trefpaffes & of vvhich
trefpaffes the apoftles tgem felues being the firft fruit of the
holie gkoaft vvere no t exempted
vvhē they faid vvee offend god in
many thinges,and if vve fay vvee
haue no finne vvee deceaue our
felues,as S.Iohn faith, amongeft
the apoftles there vvas a Iudas &
among the angels vvhich are *pu-
ri actus,*pure fpirites, and incor-
ruptible ther vvcre many that fell
among the children of Adam ,
the murtherer Cain and innoe
centAbel:euen fo among priefts,
and although there are many, by
vvhofe euill life, and vngodlie
behauiour the church fuffreth
great fcandal, yet thranxes be to
god , there are many vertuous,

P 4

Pfal. 13
52 *Eccle.*7
Prou. 10.
Iac. 1
1.*Io.*1.*Hie*
2. *Cōc. Ni-*
leni.

tuous,godlie, cōtinēt, not ytched
vvith ambition, not defiled vvith
riotousnes , not blinded vvith
couetousnes, not infected, or
spotted vvith any mortall offence, vvhose conuersation is in heauen , and vvhose glorie is the sin-
ceritie of an vndefiled conscience, vvhose continuall exercise is
the mortification of their proper
appetites,and vvhose threasure is
a soule decked, and replenished
vvith the influence of grace, and
the vertues that do follovv it , &
as S. Augustin saith *Sacerdos si Lu-*
xuriosus est, si auarus , *&c.* If the
priest be riotous , couetuous, or
proud vvhat passeth through
his handes,is not defiled , the sa-
cramentes that he handles re-

Aug.tract.
5.mloa.

mayne vnfpoted, for as the pur-
gation that the phyfition fendeth
is nothing the vvorfe for the patient, though he that miniftreth
it vnto him, be bad. fo the facra-
mentes of the lavve of grace,
vvhich are fend frō the phyfition
of our foules, by the prieft for the
curing of the difeafe therof, haue
not their vertue from the prieft,
that miniftreth them, but by the
merites of Chrieft his paffiō, that
ordained them: and as the prieftes
in the old lavve being but figures
of the priesthood of the lavve of *Deut. ij*
grace vvere obeied of the people
vnder paine of death, much more Chrieft his prieftes, should
be obeied of Chriftians, of vvhom
him felf fpoke thefe vvordes
P 5

242 *A Mnemosynum* to the

Luc. 10.

vvhosoeuer despiseth you despiseth me, and vvhoso euer heareth
you heareth me and as S. Cypriã
saith *qui Christo non credit sacerdo-*

lib.4. ep.9.

tem facienti, postea credere incipiet
sacerdoti vindicanti vvhosoeuer
that beleueth not Chrieft ordai-
ning and inftituting preefthood
he muft beleueChrieft reuenging
the quarell of prieftes, and efpe-
cialie on thofe that punifhe them
as trayturs, and banish them as
offenders.

THE SECOND BOOKE
WHEREIN THE doubteful are re-solued.

The sanctitie of those that plan-ted the catholick religion and the impietie of the impugners therof, ought to confirme our religion.

CAP. I.

WHen faith is a vertue infused by god, by vvhich vvee doe bele-ue, euerie thinge, that

god doth reueale vnto his churche, and the churche doth propose vnto the faithful to beleeue,
then Caluin, and Luder haue noe
faith, vvhen they do not beleeue
in the Catholike churche, nor in
the communion of Sainctes, &c.
for accordinge to all the diuins,
and to the holie scripturs vvhosoeuer beleeues not euerie article
of our faith, hath no faith, and
vvhen theese , do misbeleeue
moste, or all the said articles they
can haue no solid, or sounde faith
at all. Religion is nothing els
then a bindinge, and consecra-
tinge of our selues vnto god in
suche sorte, as vve should neuer
forsake him, & vvhen Luder, and
Caluine and the rest of the apost-

lés of their pretended reforma-
tion, or rather of their ovvne cō-
fufion and manifeſt deſtruction
of all religion , and pietie, haue
quite forſaken god , vnto vvhom
by folemne vovv they vvere de-
dicated,haue, forſaken their religion,haue brocken their promiſ-
ſe,haue volated, and tranſgreſſed
their ſacred vovves,and haue cau
ſed others to do the like.vve may
eaſilie perceaue that there is no
religion in them,and vvhen they
haue no religion them ſelues:
hovv may vvee become religious
by them,vvhen in their dealinges
vvee ſee nothing but all irreligious impietie:the effect of good
religion are good vvorkes according to S.Iames to viſit and ſuc-

Iac.
curre orphans, and vvidovves in
their tribulation, and to kepe him
selfe vnspotted in this vvorld,
vvhat good vvorkes may vvee ex-
pecte of these people, that do
say that all our good vvorkes are
sinnefull, that god doth not care
for them, that according to Luder
his doctrine the more detestable
a man is, the more acceptable before god, and according to Caluine, god is the authour of sinne,
and all vvickednesse, not onlie the
efficient or physical cause that
vvorketh sinne, but also the morall cause that persvvadeth it: that
vvhen sanctitie according to S.
5 Th i 2
q.61
Thomas is the flovver of religion,
vvhich is nothinh else then to offer vnto god our soule vvith all

the povvers therof vnspotted, and
voide of all filth of deadlie sinne,
and the handmaides of vvhich
sanctitie be praiers, and deuotion: *D.Th.ibid.*
by the one vve do enioy gods fa-
miliar presence: by the other vve
obtaine promptitude, and vvillin
gnesse to serue him. vvhat sancti-
tie.praiers, or deuotion may vvee
expect of them, vvhen they be
impious contemners and blasphe
mers theof, vvhen they vvith all
deuilish despight, and ragefull
tyrannie persecute not onlie the
professors therof, but also, churches, monasteries, chapples, ora-
rories and all other places vvhere
the same may be exercised, dif-
prouing, diffanulling, and despi-
fing all religiousvovves, and vota-

ries, for by folemne vovves, vvee
may become perfect feruantes of
Chrieft, and intimate vvith him,
2.*Timo*. 2. and become as it vvere dead to
this vvorld, according to the apoft
le, that fuch should not intermed
Naz.in Car le vvith any vvorldlie bufines
ad Hele. and according to. S. Nazianzen
vvhich do fegregate them felues
from the conuerfation of this
vvorld, and do côfecrate their liues vnto god, vvhich beinge eleuated aboue the earth, and being
vvithout vvife or children, their
intentiue care is to vvorship, and
honour god vvith hymnes , and
prayers both day , and night, & in
another place he faid fpeaking of
thofe religious people, thefe haue nothing to doo vvith this
vvorld,

and yet haue all thinges therin,
vvhich are the lordes of the *Ora* 1.*in*
Iul.
vvorld, thefe I fay for their mortification are immortale, and for
their litle medling vvith the
vvorld, are ioyned vnto god, and
for their folitarineffe in the fame
do embrace the ioy of the other
vvorld. this farre Naz. and althoughe many vvicked apoftates
haue abufed this facred inftitu-
tion, by rūning out of it (as Luder
and Caluine and the reft of their
apoftles, and teachers of their irreligious doctrine haue don) that
makes not the religion bad, but
rather good: no more then the 9.
orders of angellicall Hierarchie
for that lucifer and the reft of his
follovvers, through priede fell

from it, nor the apostolique order of Chrieft, for that Iudas throughe couetousnes, runne out of it, nor the mercie of god, the vvorſe though it be abuſed by preſumptnous ſinners, vvho are the more prone to ſinne, becauſe god is mercifull. and trulie if ther vvere no other reaſon to cõfirme and proue our holie catholick religion, then that ſuch deteſtable, and abhominable apoſtates, ſo vicious in their liues, ſo impious and blaſphemous in their doctrine, ſo variable vncertaine and faythleſſe in their fayth, ſo confuſed in their procedings, vvho vvithout order auctoritie or apoſtolicke ſpirit or commiſſion licentiouſlie, and excurſiuelie do range abroad prea-

ching their irreligious herefies
condemned, reiected, and ana
thematized by all generall councels, and fpecialie by the famous
authenticall generall councell of
Trente, vvhichvvas an affembly
of all the patriarches, Archbif-
hops, bifhops, prelates, generales
of holie orders, Abbotes, doctors,
and diuins of all Chriftiendome,
fhould (I fay) ympugne and dif-
proue the fame, it fhould be an
euident argumente to confound
the heretick and confirme the
catholicke.

Novve let vs come vnto the
apoftles that did firft plant our
catholick religion in Irelãd, fome
authoures do vvrite that S. Iames
Mãior vvas in Ireland, being by

vvind driuen thither, Paladius the

popes legate (as Cæsar Baronius
vvitnesseth) did preach in Irelād
and after vvardes Sainct Patrick
vvas set thither by Celestinus pope as the saidBar. declareth anno Christi 431. num. 191. Gige-
bertus in chronica, vvho vvith
an a apostolicall spirit, feruent
prayers, long fasting, austere mortification, sharpe discipline, religious obseruation of all spirituall
perfection, and feruent charitie,
did subdue that kingdom vnto
the standarte of the crosse & the
svveet yoke of Chriest his lavves,
his most holie life, and the strāge
vvounders and miracles, that god
did vvorke by him, vvas an euident vvitnesse that his doctrine

vvas of god. othervvise hovv
could a poore soule void of all
hmaine forces, and vvorldlie pollicies subdue in one quarter of a
yeare, a borbarous, vicious and vn
tractable nation vnto such hard
lavves, both vnto our capacitie
vn reasonable, and vnto fleash
and blood yrcksom and intolle-
rable, vnlesse god vvhose vvorke
he had in hand, had holpen and
cooperat vvithim, by strange miracles, both vvounderfull to be
seene, and ympossible to be don
by humaine povver. vvhat is more dissonant to our grosse sensible
iudgment and knovvledge, then
that Christ should be the sonne
of a virgine, and rhat he vvas god
and man, and that being god,

Q 3

vvhofe nature is immortall, and
ympaffible should die, should be
crucified as a theefe, should be
dead and buried , & and that the
fame god is he,that vvee receaue,
vnder the vaile of accidentes of
bread and vvine in the eucharift,
that being fed vvith Chrieft, vvee
may be purified and fanctified by
him,and that Chrieft according
to his deitie is one vvith the father, and the holie ghoft vnited
in one nature, fubftance or effen-
ce and perfection , only diftinct
and different from god the father
and the holie ghoft in certaine
notions , perfon , or hypoftafis:
and that the bodie being conuerted vnto ashes muft appeare before Chrieft , that vvas fo cruci-

hed by man to receaue according
to his desertes. vvhat is more
loathsom vnto fleash, and blood,
then to be crucified and mortified, vnto this vvorlde, and to be
depriued of all corruptible appetites therof, to follovve Chrieft
crucified, to vvalke in the ftreight
narrovve vvay of his croffe, and to
defpife deteft & abhore the broad
vvay of the licentious doctrine
of thefe heretixes, for if vve leaue of our fayth, vvhich according
to S. Gregorie hath no merite
vvhen humane reafon giueth experience, the doctrine of thofe
apoftates is more agreable vnto
our fenfes and more conformable
vnto fleash and blood, and more
pleafant vnto our corrupt nature,

vvhich inclineth to follovve licē-
tious libertie,and the vvorᴋes of
darcknesse,vvhichare voluptuous
pleasures,beastlie concupiscence,
vvithout any restrainct of any spirituall lavve,vvithout obseruatiō
of vovves: vvithout any regard of
the sacrament of pennance & the
3.essentiall partes therof, as contrition,confession,and satisfactiō,
vvhich is the onlie medicine ordained by Chriest to cure & heale the vvoundes of ourpoore soule corrupted and lāguished vvith
sinne,vvithout any deuotiō or res
pect to any religion, religious ceremonies,sacrisices and sacramē-
tes, churches, and oratories ordained by our ancetoures for the
seruice of god:all vvhich they do

deſtroy, vvher they haue any poa
vver: and in ſteed therof, do ende-
uoure to plante a negatiue reli-
giou, vvhich according to the
phploſopher eſt *malignãtis natu-*
ræ quicquid ante ſe inuenit deſtruit:
is of a malignant nature vvhatſoeuer it findeth beſor, it doth
destroye the ſame, for ther is no
religion, order, obſeruation, that
the church of god had at any time but this infernall hereſie laboreth to abolish aud overtrovve
it quite.

Novv hauing hearde and to
your greateſt griefe felt the vvorkes and endeauoures of Luder, &
Caluine: vvherin they applied
them ſelues, I thought good to
ſpeaĸe a litle of our cuntrie

Q 5

sainctes vvhose zeale, charitie, ho-
linesse of life many nations vvere
conuerted vnto the faith of
Chriest. of vvhich I vvill put dovvne some fevv examples, if
if vvee may beleue venerable Beda that did vvrite the life of S.
Patrick and of other sainctes of
Irland (said) that they vvere a mi-
rour and spectacle of all religious
Beda lib. 3. perfection. and sanctitie. of S. Co-
ca. 4. histo- lumbanus he vvriteth thus. Co-
Angli. lumbanus came out of Ireland in
his habite, and life a famous mõ-
cke to preach christian religion,
vnto the Pictes Meilochon being
a most mightie king of that nation sthe yeare of our lorde 565.
and conuerted that nation by
vvorde and example vnto the

fayth of Chrieſt before he vvas
come into England, he founded
a moſt famous monaſterie in Ireland, vvhich for the abundanceof
oxes, is called in the Irish tonge
deragh that is to ſay the fielde of
oackes out of vvhich monaſteries
many other monaſteries vvere
made by his diſciples in England
and Ireland. the ſame doth Cæſar
Baro. confirme. In Ireland ſayth
the ſaid Beda many noble and
meane people vvhen Finan and
Colman vvere bishops ther, de-
parting out of England for ob-
taininge of diuine knovledge and
for embracing a côtinent life : ſome did enter into religion, conſe-
crating them ſeluas vnto the ſer-
uice of almightie god : others did

anno Chri-
ſti 365.nu.
30. Bed.lib.
3. 27. hiſt.
anno Chri-
ſti. 64.

labour to get and purchase knovvledge, and science, for vvhom
Irishmen most gladlie erected se
minaries furnishing them vvith
booxces, and all other necessaries
for their purpose vvithot money
or revvarde. this farre venerable
Beda of the charitie of Ireland
tovvardes Englisme. S. ʙern. also

D. Ber. in
vita
B. Malach.

in the life of S. Malach. bishop of
lismore saith that ther vvas a monasterie in Irelād vvhich vvas the
mother of many thousand mona
steries, he added also a most holie
place & fertle of sainctes , vvhich
most abūdātlie did fructifie vnto
god so as one of the children of
that holie monasteries erected
100. monasteries: of this vvee may
gather hovv many vvere the rest,

that Ireland, yelded ſo as S.Ber.
ſaith:the verſe of Dauid vnto
Ireland may be applied *viſitaſti
terram & inebriaſti eam multipli-
caſti eam*: *o lord* thovve haſt viſi-
ted the earth thoue haſt ovver-
flovve it vvith ſanctitie and
thou haſt abundantlie enriched
the ſame vvith holineſſe, and the
ſvvaremes of ſactes did not onlie
multiplie in Ireland, and in the
contries adioyning, but alſo they
made theit inundatiō into exter-
nall nations, of vvhich Columbanus came into our pattes of
France, and made the monaſterie of Luxouia ſo great and
ſo religious, that the qui-
er therof vvas neuer any
moment both day and night

vvithout prayſing of god. thus farre, S. Bern. of the religion of Ireland, vvhich calleth S. Malachias a ſecond Moyſes, and a ſecond Aaron, vvho vvas a ſufficient vvitneſſe of his life, and death, for he died vvith him in his monaſterie of Clareuall, vvhoſe bodie is keipt there vntill this day as amoſt precious relicke, vvhat shall I ſaye of the bleſſed S. Romoaldas the king of Ireland his ſonne Atchbishop of Mekline in Flanders and Patrone of that cuntrie, of Dymna the king of Leinſter his daughter, that vvas martyred in Flåders, of S. Folianus the brother of holie Furſeus the apoſtle of Auſtria, of holie Brandon that hath conuetted vnto Chriſt ſo many Ilandes in

the Ocean fea, and fome of them
this day are called the Ilandes of
S.Brandon fo holie in his life and
fo miraculous in vvorkes, that it is
avvounder fo heare therof: of the
3 fonnes of Vrbian king of Itelād
vvhich vvere called Froſeus, Folianus, and Vltauus all bleſſed ſan-
ctes, vvhich ann.DCL.came into
France and vvere receaued moſt
courteouslie of King Clodoueus
and obtained of him licenſe to
erect a monaſterie in France, vvhat ſhall I ſpeake of
Killian of vvhom Laurentius Surius ſpeaketh thus, Killian of the
ſcotiſh nation, trulie I mean Ireland, it is a fertile Iland in the O-
cean fea but more fertile of Sainctes and holie men of vvhich Ira-

*Platb. de
bono ſtatus
religioſi lib
2.c.7*

*apud Taxu
i imiac.*

lic reioyceth for Columbanus, Germanie is enriched vvith Gallus, France is renovvmed for Killian.vvhich did suffer martyrdome and conuerted vnto the fayth all Languedock and the cuntris adioyning. this farre Surrius.thiese godlie people in nothing did labour so much, as in conuerting soules vnto god, by mortifieng their bodies, by shevving vertuous examples of good life vnto all those vvith vvhome they did conuerse,for Ireland in multitude of sanctes, in austeritie of life, in heauenlie conuersation, vvas not inferioure to any natiõ in the vvorld, exceipt for martyrdome. the reason vvherof the Archbushopp of Cashall beinge demaũ-

of Geraldus Cambrensis secre-
tarie to king Iohn in Ireland,
vvherfore Ireland hauing so
manysanctes,yeelded no martyrs,
did shevv, that Irish people, although they vvere barbaro', yet
vvould neuer embrevv their handes vvith the blood of such people: but novve (saith he)vvhen
you are come among vs. vve shall
notvvant martyrs,truelie you haue had of late dayes constant mar
tyrs,as you cānot be ignorāt therof, and perhaps ere long you
may haue more , if your persecution shallcontinue,and also if you
be as resolute, and determined to
perseuere in your anciēt faith, as
your persecutors be cruell to trye
your patience by the effusion

R

of your blood.this is the time of
your merit, by your sufferance,
novve you are brought vnto the
fielde of yourcombat,& vnto the
skirmish of yout coronatiō,if you
be deteimined to dye,rather then
to make a shipvvracke of your
faith,vvhich haue brought forth
so many blessed sainctes of your
ovvne nation, by vvhose godlie
example your faith is confirmed,
yourcoūtrie renovvmed,and god
glorified.hold it for certaine that
thiese holie people and the broo-
de of Caluine can neuer take rest
in oneKingdome,Iacob and Esau
could neuer agree. and although
they had one father called Isaac
and Rebeca to their mother, yet
they neuer possesfled one inheri-

tance,nor enioyed one patrimonie,& although they vvere in o-
ne belly,and vvere borne at one
time, yet they haue not one hea
uen,Iacob for obeing his mother *Exod. 32.*
had the benedictiō of the father,
vvho praiedvnto god,that his po-
fteritie should multiplie as the
fandes of the fea, thiefe bleffed
fainctes forobeing the catholicke
church,vvhich fignified Rebecca
haue the fatheres benediction, &
are multiplied as the fandes of
the fea & the ftarres of heauen.
vvhat are the vertuous religious
gentlemé,that defpife the vvorld,
forfake lādes and great poffeffiōs,
deny them felues. and embrace
the croffe of our fauiour in humilitie, in voluntarie pouertie, per-

R 2

fect obedience, and perpetuall
continencie,but the posteritie of
these blessed sainctes is the fruite
of this benediction,and the effect
of their religion.seeing that euery
cause is knovven by his effect, e -
uerie tree by his fruit, and the
faith of euery Christian by his
charitie,vve must thinke that the
catholicke religion is the onlie
true religion,that procureth such
heroicall resolutions in mens bre
stes,by vvhich they be so austere
in their mortification, so mortified in their passiõs,so euangelical
in their conuersatiõ,and so chari-
table in their vvorkes: of vvhich
vve haue many blessed examples:
vvas that not agreat charitie of F.
Thomas vvhit naturall of Clõmel

feing many poore fcholers of his
nation in great miferie in Valo-
dolid in Caftile hauing no means
to continue their ftudie, no r language to begge, hauing giuen o-
uer his ovvne priuate commodi-
tie, did recollect & reduce thē to
one place, vvhich he mayntained
by his induftrie and begging, vntil by his petition to Phillip the
fecond anno domini 1593. a col-
ledge of Irish ftudentes vvas
founded. the like charitie f. Iohn
Huling naturall of vvexford did
exercife in Lisborne, for by his induftrie, and the charitie of godlie
people didl releue a cetaine
nomber of Irîsh youthes and in
the time of plague in Lisborne
fought licence of his fuperiour to

R 3

ſerue in the hoſpital of the plague vvherof he dyed.vvhich vvas
a ſufficient ſigne of his great charitie. maſter Chryſtopher Cuſake
did imitate thieſe good people,
for he being cō vnto Flanders to
ſtudie,and finding manyvertuous
youthes of his natiō of ripe vvitte
and ſharpe iudgment, not able to
go forvvard in their learning , for
vvant of exhibition:did giue vnro
them vvhat money he had,as alſo
did giue ouer his intēded purpoſe
of ſtudie , & by his induſtrie
great chatihe and begging
ſuſtayneth,100 poore ſcollers in
Flandersꞇ vvho vvill not admire
the charitie of S.MorrisKēt prieſt
naturall of Kill maluck, vvho pu-
blickly appeered before S. Iohn

Norrice then lorde prefident of
Munfter, to redeeme his hofte m.
Victor vvhit of Cloamell out of
prifon; in vvhich he vvas Kept by
the faid L. Prefident for Keping
the faid prieft in his houfe, ma-
fter vvhit vvas enlarged and his
gueft vvas hanged and quartered:
this great charitie cannot come
but from a good faith. thiefe ex-
extraordinarie vvorckes do declare a found religion. thiefe be
they that are ordayned vt *comple-
tentur muri Hierufalim* to make
vp the number of fuch that are
appo nted for Hierufalim. fo as
by this means you may perceeae
vvhither thiefe bleffed people or
the vkhelps of Caluine haue the
true catholick and apoftolick religion.   R   4

THE CONTINVANCE

of our religion in Ireland almost these 1102. by lauufull, & apostolicke succession, is an euident proof that it is the right catholicke religion.

CAP. II.

D.th 6uad
l. 2.ar.15
Scot.in 4.d
13.q 2. Pa
lud omuis
Adria. g.
de proseri-
ptione Soto
4.deiust q
S. Medi.co-

IT is decreed, and ennacted by all cānon, and ciuil lauves that vvhosoeuer possesseth any land or immoueable goodes the

space of. 20. or. 30. yeers vvhich is
the greateſt time that any lavv
doth giue, that ſo long a poſſeſſiõ
doth preſcribe, viz. that he is the
right ovvner and lord of the ſame
of vvhich he hath the poſſeſſion,
ſo as he be *poſſeſſor bonæ fidei.* 1.
bonæ conſcientiæ that is to ſay,
that he is certaine all that time of
the iuſt title theof, to be his, and
none els during that time
should haue any clayme, or iuſt
chalenge thervnto, and if after
that time of. 20. or. 30. yeers any
clayme, or challenge be made a-
gainſt any ſuch landes poſſeſſed
bona fide ſo long time, though
the ſaid challẽge be neuer ſo iuſt,
it cannot remoue the defendant
from his poſſeſſion, and he may

d ce de reſti.
Canno. 16.
q 3. ex can
no. ſi virgo
cap finali
de preſcrip
lege pri-
made ff. de
vſucupion

R 5

vvith a safe conscienceKeepe the
said lādes, or any such immouable
thing, and this is called prescrip-
siō. if it be mouable thing, the said
lavves do giue no more then. 4.
yeers and this is called vsucapio.
vvhen vvee haue possessiō of our
religion 1202. yeers from posteritie to posteritie, from councel to
councell, from age to age, vvhich
vvas fortold by the oracles of the
prophets, that vvas signified by
the faith of the Patriarkes, vvhich
vvas declared and deliuered vnto
vs by the creed and preaching of
teh apostles, vvhichvvas sealed by
the blood of so many millions of
martyrs, vvhichvvas beautified by
vovves of so many blessed virgi-
nes vvhic vvas established by mi-

racles and vvunders , vvhich vvas
by charitie increafed ,'by the iugement,and fentences of the vni-
uerfall catholicke chutch defined
by the decrees,and definitiōs of
allSainctes,and generall councels
approved,by the mutuall andvni-
forme confent of all natiós tried,
by the|cōuerfiō of allKingdomes
and prouinces made Knovven, &
illumined,by the heretickes of all
ages impugned,and perfecuted,&
by their perfecution made firme
perfect, and ftedfaft, and vvhich
by the lavvfull, and continuall
fucceffion of Popes and bishops
from.S.Peter vnto Paulus 5. that *Au.epiſto-*
novv raignes confirmed:if S.Aug. *la 165 &*
only by the fucceffion of S. Peter *42 Item*
vntoAnaftafiùs that vva s Pope in *c.4*
contra epi
ſtolā funda

his time did proue the catholicke
religion to be in the church of
Rome.if S.Ambrose did proue it
from S. Peter vnto Damasus : if

Cypr. lib 1 S.Cypriā did proue it frō S.Peter
ep 6 Ber li vnto Fabian,and Cornelius, if S.
3 de consid
ad Eu Am Bernard did proue it from S. Pe-
fup 1 Ts 3 ter vnto Eugenius,if euerie one of
them did proue it by apostolicke
succeſſiō from.S.Peter vnto their
time,haue not vvee greater reaſō
to beleue our catholick religion
to be at Rome, and from thence
to come vnto our cuntrie and vnto other places of Europe by a-
poſtolick and oderlie succeſſion,
iſſuing from the ſame church, if
vvee can shevve the ſame succeſſion, from S. Peter vnto Paulus
Quintus novvePope,for vve haue

no other religion then that , that
S.Patrick brought from Rome:of
vvhich thanckes be to our rede-
mer vvee haue the poffeffion al-
moft 1202 thoughe vvee be of late yeeres by Luder and Caluin
and by their follovvers difturbed,
and difquieted therin. vvill not
you accout him a vvragler , and a
troublefom mate,that vvould go
about to take a vvay your liuing
from you,of vvhich yon haue not
only the poffeffion , but alfo the
iuft title therof avovvched vnto
you by the verdit of all the iuries
of Ireland,and cofirmed vnto you
by the generall decree of all fta-
tutes, and courtes of parlement
of the fame,but our religio being
confirmed vnto vs by all the ge-

generall parlementes not only of
oneKingdom,but of allChristen-
dom,ought to be vnto vs vndoubt
full,and certaine,and all such ma
tes to be reputed for vvranglers,
that do endeauour to take yt frō
vs,forvvhich this late persecution
is intended.but I vvould theyhad
follovved the graue counsell of

Act. 5 Gamaliel,vvho being consulted
vvithall,by theIevves concerning
the apóstles and christians, that
vveare at Hierusalem:said if they
vveare not of god , they should
shortlie come to nothing as many
false prophetes (said he)gaue vn
to vs experience,and if they be of
god in Kaine you striue against
them,be cause ther is no counsell,
nor pollicie saieth the holie gost

againſt god vvhich doth ouer-
throvve the counſell of ſinners.
our religion ſactifice, ſacramēt &
preeſthood is of Chrieſt and ther
fore the force of man cannot preuaile againſt it if. by the prophe-
cie of Malachias, there muſt be a
ſacrifice offered vnto god alvvaies
and in euerie corner of the vvorld
vvhich vvas not meāt of the ſacrifice of the old lavve, for by many
places of ſcripture that ſacrifice
could not be offered but at Hie-
ruſalē, therfore it muſt be verified
of the ſacrifice of the maſſe,
vvhich is the ſacrifice of all ſacrifices, for vvhich Chrieſt hath ordained prieſtes, vvhen he ſaid do
this in remembrance of me; vnto
vvhom S. Paul, ſaid, they could

Prou. 28
pſ. 3 *Hſb*
7 *Luc* 26
1. *Cor.* 11
Conc.Trid
Malach. 1
Dent 14.
24 & 26
1 *para.* 17
11 & 22.
& 2 *para*
6 & *pſal.*
77 68 69
Iob. c: 4
Iuc 22. 1
Cor ii 10.

not drinck the chalice of Chrieſt,
and the deuill, and conſequentlie
this ſacrifice muſt be offered by
prieſtes in Ireland, vvhich according to the ſaid Malachias are An
gells of god, that muſt offer ſacrifice, and shall applie the vniuerſall ſacrifice of Chrieſt vnto our
particulier miſeries, and calamities: for as vniuerſall cauſes neuer
vvorke vnles they be applied by
particuler cauſes, by vvhich they
be determined : ſo the oblatiõ of
the ſacrifice of Chrieſt though it
vvas a ſufficient expiation for all
our offences, yet being an vniuerſall cauſe muſt be applied by particuler cauſes to vvorke his effect

That

THAT THE PRIMA-cie of this church, by vvhich the apostolike succession, and continuance therof is establi-shed vvas founded by Chriest, reason and auctoritie confirming the same.

CAP. III.

I N all thinges vvee see a subordination of an in-feriour, to a superiour: in the celestiall, and an-gelicall Hierarchie the inferiour order concerning their intellectu

S

call operation or supernaturall
reuelation, do depēd of the superiour, vvhich are called Archan-
gels, euerie corpulent substance
in his corporall motion depen-
deth of a supreme bodie, vvhich
is called (*primum mobile*) : amon
gest lightsome bodies, the sunne
hath the preeminence , vvithout
vvhose influence, no such thing
hath any light : so as there is nothing in this vvorld according to
the philosopher, and as experiēce teacheth , that is not reduced
vnto his Kinde, by vvhich the perfection therof is measured: amongest sensible creatures the reasonable creature vvhich is man , is
the chiefest , by vvhich euerie
such liuingthing is measured a-

mongeſt Chriſtians, Chrieſt according his humane nature, hath
a ſupreame iuriſdiction *de cuius*
plenitudine nos omnes accepimus of
vvhom vve depend in our ſupernaturall being. vvhy ſhould not
in the church of god this order
be obſerued, that there ſhould be
one church, by vvhoſe direction
all churches ſhould be gouerned
&by vvhich all churches ſhould
be tried and ordered: ſo among
the apoſtles there vvas. S. Peter
vvhich made the firſt profeſſion
of our fayth on vvhō the ſuperio-
ritie vvas inſtituted, and the chur
che founded. as vppon a firme *Math 16.*
rocke Chrieſt ſpeaking vnto him,
thou arſt a rock and vppon this *Math 17.*
Luc 12.
roc ke vvill I build my churck, &
S   2

I. 01.

the gates of hell shall not preuaile againſt it, &c. *Tu es* as S.
Hieron. expounded vpon thee,
&vnto thee I vvill giue the *Keies*
of the Kingdome of heauen this
authoritie is confirmed by many
prerogatiues, and priuileges that
he hath in the gospell, that chriſt
did pay the tribute for him ſelf
and S. Peter, vvhere he praied that
S. Peters fayth, should neuer faile
in the vvorld, vvhere he ſaied vnto
S. Peter thou being once confirmed ſtrengthen thy brethren: of
the ſucceſſors of S. Peter this is
demanded (ſaith S. Bernard,) that
Chriſt commended vnto him
thrice the feeding of his flocke, alſo the authoritie he hath in the
actes. this primacie of S. Peter is

Marc Vlt.

Math 17
Lucis
Io 20

Ber: p. 190

Actorum
1.2.3.4 5.
6.8.9.11.15

auouched, and approued by S. Cyprian by S.Hieron.by S.Amb. by S.Chryf.by S.Aug.contra *Ep. Donati* by S. Hilarie vppon S. Math. by S.Leo in the anniuerfarie fermon:by S.Greg. *in moralib. & in regiftro ad Mauritium Aug.* by S.Cyp.*de fimplicitate prælatorũ* by S.Aug.in his queft: of the nevve and old teftamĕt byS.Leo fer: *afce.Dominic. Bed.in homi Ath. in Ep.ad Marcũ Liber. Fœli:Euf. Cæf. laĉt, Paul, Anfel.*

Cyp. lib. 4 epift.ad Pa piand & lib.1. ad Coruel O- rig. Sup. Mat. Hier. lib 1.Pelag & in fer.d Petro ad Amb.in fer 47 Chryf fu- per Io 8& eomi fup Math.

Firft the faith vvas taught in Iudea,and fo came vnto Samaria and to other places, omitting the eaft and the fouth,it is certaine that S. Peter did fend vnto Germany to teach the faith Crefcĕtes, Eucharius , and Valerius,

Aĉtor. 1.8 & Heb.2 6

vnto France he fent Sixtus. Sini-
tius, Amanfius, Mennius, and Mar-
tialis, and S. Clement did fend Dio
nyfius Areopagita vvith Rufticus
Eleutherus, Sactinus. Exuperius,
and Eutropius vnto Paris and
Guyen. the reft of S. Pe. fucceffors
did fend in all ages paftors vnto
other partes of the vvorld to conuert them vnto the faith, vnto
Eng. Eleuth the Pope did fend S.
Getmanus in the time of Lucius
King of Kent, aftervvard by S.
Greg. vvere fent vnto England
holie monckes S. Aug. and his brethren to reclaime England for
that it fell from the firft faith, as
S. Patrick and Paladius by Sceleft:
vnto Ireland & Scotlãd & as thefe
days many are fent vnto the eaft

and vveaſt, South, and North by
S. Peters ſucceſſors, ſo as no nation vvas euer, conuerted but by
the lavvfull miſſion of S. Peter,&
his ſucceſſors, vnto vvhō Chrieſt
committed the charge and feeding of his Flocke; vve neuer red,
that any natiō vvas brought vnto
Chrieſt by heretickes, ſauing the
Goathes vvhich vveare conuerted or rather ſubuerted, by the Ar
rians, & did not continue therin.
this care and charge of feeding of
Chrieſt his flocke, vvas not onlie
committed vnto S. Peter, but alſo
vnto his ſucceſſors, othervviſe
Chrieſt had no care of his flocke
nor of hiſi church, but during. S.
Peter his time, and he being dead
this charge aud gouernmēt of his

church vvas ended vvith him,
vvhich should be abfurd to thincke,vvhen his church muft continue to the vvorldes end.

for if the church should not haue
a head vnder Chrieft, by vvhofe
order&direⅿió the fame shoulde
be prudētlie gouuerned,it shoulde,be a bodie vvithout a head, a
flockevvithout apaftour,a church
vvithout a vicar, a multitude vvithout vnitie, vvhich being vvithout any fubordinatió of an infe
riour to a lavvfull fuperiour,is no
thing els, then a chaos vvithout
order,and a certaine confufion of
a popular tumulte vvithout orderlie direⅿion or difcretion,and
if the church of god be one as it
is faid in the canticles *vna eft colū-*

ba mea perfecta mea , vna est matri sua, my doue is one , the mother hath but one daughter, perfectiō of loue consisteth in vnitie, all this vnitie is spoken of the church of Chrieft, vvithout vvhich vnitie it could not be called *caftrorum acies ordinata* an armye vvell trayned, a battaile vvell ordered , and if chrieft praiedvnto his father that his flockе should be one , and S. Paul faieth that hischurch should be one bodie mifticall , fo there should be faieth he one fpirit to quicкen it, one lord to direct it, one faith to vvalke therin, & one baptifme to clenfe it , that vvee should not faieth he, bevvauering in our faith like enfantes and lead avvay vvith euerie vvind of do-

Can. 6

Ibid. 6

Ioh. 17

Eph. 4

S 5.

&rine in the vvickednesse of men
in subtilitie through deceit of errour, and turbulent spirits, hovv
can this vnitie of faith , vnitie of
direction, vnitie of spirit be pre-
seruedvvhere one is not admitted
to gouerne,& vvhere euerie ones
fantasticall spirit, and furious pas
sion, is his leader & directour· for
preuenting of vvhich inconue-
niēce. it is necessarie there should
be in the church of god one mo-
deratour, one iudge, & one head,
by vvhich the bodie and mēbers
therof should be directed, and as
S.Bernard saieth as in heauen Ar-
changels, and angels seraphins, &
cherubins are disposed vnder one
head, vvhich is god : so also here
vnder one bishop , be primates,

S.Bern.lib.
9. de couns.
ad Eug.

Patriarches, Archibishops, bishops, prieftes, abates vvith the
reft, vvhich head in hovv many
places of his boockes doth he call
the bishop of Rome, and as S. *Cyl.4.epa*
Cyp. faieth euerie kingdō hathhis
feuerall king, euerie people, cittie,
tovvne, village, houfe, & fo forth
haue their feuerall head or gouer-
nour ergo. the vvhole church *lib.de vnita*
te Eccl ep. 2.
vvhich is but one diuided vnto *1 ep. 3 ep. 8*
& in ep. ad
many members, muft haue one *quintus*
head afvvell as hath one Kingdome, one people, one cittie. and in
other places he faieth as in Earth
many riuers haue one fpring, many branches one roote, many mēbers one bodie & one head: therfore faith he in the mifticall bodie of Chrieft there is one head

to rule the fame, vvhich he faieth

Aug lib 1 cont Iou to be S. Peter *quem Dominus* (faieth he) *optimũ elegit fuper quẽ ædi-
ficauit ecclefiã fuã* vvhich our lord
hath chofen to be the firſt vpõ
vvhom he builded his church
Aug ibide & as S. Aug. faieth *vnus eligitur inter 1 2. capite conſtituto fcifmatis tol-
latur occafio* amongeſt 1 2. one is
chofen to take avvay all occafion
of fchifme and diuifion. the effect
of vvhich vnitie, and iurifdiction
by ordayning of one head vve fee
in the'church ofRome, by vvhich
all fchifme, and herefie vvas taken
avvay. vvas not the Arriã and the
Pelagian herefie taken avvay by
this auctoritie, vvas not Ireland
among other countries abfolued
from the Pelagian herefie by the

churche of Rome as Cef. Baro.
vvriteth Irish bishops (faith this
authour)touching their faith or
rather oppreffed vvith troubles
do fubmit thē felues vnto S.Gre
gorie vvhofe anfvver vnto them I
thought good to put dovvne.

*Bar anno
chr 360 10
5 8 6*

*The copie of S.Greg.his epift. vn-
to the bishops of Irelād many of them being infected
vvith the pelagian herefie.*

SCripta veſtra ſumma cum gratu-
latione ſuſcepi,ſed erit in me vbe-
rior valdè lætitia,ſi mihi de veſtra
contigerit reuerſione gaudere. prima
itaque epiſtolæ veſtræ frons, graues
vos pati perſecutiones innotuit , quæ

*D Greg li
2 epiſto 3 b
induſtione
1 a*

quidem perſecutio dum non rationa-
biliter ſuſtinetur, nequaquam proficit
ad ſalutem. nam nulli fas eſt retribu-
tionem præmiorum expectare pro cul-
pa. debetis. n. ſcire (ſicut D. Cypr. dixit)
quia martyrem non facit pæna, ſed
cauſa: dum igitur ita ſit, incongruum
nimis eſt de ea quam dicitis perſecu-
tione gloriari per quam vos conſtat ad
æterna premia minime prauehi. redu-
cat ergo charitatem veſtram tandem
integritas fidei ad matrem quæ vos
generauit eccleſiam: nulla perſuaſio
vos a recto itinere defatiget, nulla vos
animorum intentio a concordiæ vni-
tate diſſociet. quod autem ſcribitis
quia ex illo tempore inter alias pró-
uincias maxime flagellatur Italia: nō
hoc ad eius debetis retorquere oppro-
brium. quoniam ſcriptum eſt quem di-

ligit Dominus castigat, flagellat au-
tem omnem filium quam recipit; si igi-
tur ita est, vt dicitis eo tempore magis
dilecta apud Deum & modis omnibus
approbata, ex quo Domini sui meruit
sustinere flagella. I am made ioyfull
for receauinge your letters, but I
shalbe more ioyfull, if I shall heare of your conuersion. by the pre-
amble therof I vnderstãd that you
suffre a heauie persecutiõ, vvhich
if it be not accordinglie sustained
auayleth nothing for your iustifi-
cation. none should expect a revvard, vvhen his demerites de-
sherue punishmẽt, you ought to
Knovv as S. Cyprian faith paine
maketh not the martyr, but the
cause, therfore it is not conueniẽ
that you should glory in that per

secution, by vvhich you cannot
arriue at the Kingdome of heavē.
let the integritie of your faith reduce you vnto your mother
church that ingendred you:let no
opiniōs disioine you from the vni
tie of concord:let no persuasiō
or vvearinesse cause you to forgo
the right vvay.& that vvhich you
vvrite of Italie to be afflicted amō
gest other prouinces you ought
not to obiect the same vnto it as a
reproch, be cause it is vvrittē god
chastisethvvhom he loueth,for he
vvhippeth euerie sonne, that he
receaueth, seeing as your selues do vvrite that then he beginneth to be godes electe vvhen he
sustayneth gods crosses and affli-
ctions.this farre S. Greg.vnto the
bishops

bishops of Ireland being infected vvith the pelagiã errour, of vvhich being fore afflicted they fought abfolution firft of Pelagius the Pope: but the fame vvas not effectuallie don vntill S. Greg. did it. *Deut.* 17.

Verie reafon vvithout auctorie of Chrieft or his fainctes should perfuade vs., that there should be in the church of god this principalitie. in the old lavve therevvas a high prieftvvhofe cõmandement vvas obeied, and vvhofe rule vvas efteemed, and byvvhofe order the finagoge vvas directed & as Moyfes vvas carefull therof: vvhy should not Chrieft prouide for his ovvne fpoufe.

And although by nature vvee *Luk.2.mora* be all equall yet as S. Greg. faieth

T

by the secret vvorke and dispen-
sation of. nature it self one hath
more merite then another, and so
more preheminence. vve see one
more rude & lūpish thē another,
vvhich should be directed, by one
that hath his iugemēt more ripe,
his vnderstāding more prōpt, and
his experiēce more perfect; & so
Plato lib. 3 de rep. Plato saieth thatvvoemen are the
seruantes of men, because ordina-
rilie theybe not so capable of gouerment or sovvell able to manage vveightie affaires.

　Chriest therfore being a proui-
dent spouse for his church, to the
end that order may duelie be obserued therin, hath cōmitted our
charge to one, by vvhose ordervve
should be directed , by vvhose

vvatche vvee should be defended
from the vvolues, and by vvhofe
holie doctrinevvee should be fed:
but the hereticke (as S. Gregorie
faieth) to take avvay this order frõ
gods church, barketh againft the
cheif paftor, that it may fall out,
as it did among the Ifraelits, vvhẽ
they had no King: euerie one did
vvhat liked him beft: and therfore
as S. Aug. faieth, *fupremus paftor* *Aug lib cõ-*
ad impiorum detruncationem gladio *tra collato-*
petri dexteras omnium armauit *rem ca.41.*
antiftitum the paftour did arme *Aug lib 3*
the right hãd of all bishops vvith *contr ep pa-*
Peters fvvord to the cutting of *lag*
vvicked mẽ, and therfore he faid *Aug cõtra*
that he hadthe preeminẽce in the *dona & pag*
bishoplie care aboue all others *4*
againft vvhom the proud gates of

hell should neuer preuaile, this is
the church saieth he *in qua semper*

Epist.16i.c. 4 contra *viguit principalitas, &c.* the principalitie of apostolicke chaire euer

Epist. fund florished: this is the church saieth
he that in all the vvorld may cha-

Cyp.lib.i ep 6 ad ma- gnad Math:18 Cyp lib 4 ep 8 lenge vnto her self this vvorde
catholicke, vvithout vvhose au-
ctoritie he vvould not haue beleue the gospell. this is the church
according to S. Cypr. that vvhosoeuer vvould not obey, should
be holden as an ethnicke, this
church of Rome he called *catho-*

Aug de Fi- de ad l'etre *licæ fidei radicem & matricem* the
root & mother of the catholicke
faith: this is the church according
to S. Hierom, that vvhosoeuer
vvould eat the lambe out of it
should be prophane : this is the

church saieth S. Auguſt. vvithout
vvhich neyther baptiſme norvvor
kes of mercie can do vs good.
this is the church of vvhich the
generall councel of Chalcedõ hauing receaued letters frõ Rome
ſaied theſe ✦vordes· *hæc eſt patrum* Chal act 2
fides. hæc apoſtolorum fides: ita omnes
credimus. anathema ſit, qui ita nõ cre
dit:this is the faith of our fathers
&c. this is the faithof the councel
of Florẽce vvherin the Greciãs&
Armeniãs did forgoe their old er
roures, & ſubmitted them ſelues
vnto the church of Rome, did de-
cree ſpeaking after this maner *dé-* Concilium
finimus ſanctam apoſtolicã ſedẽ,&c. Flo Roffen
vve do define & decree that the ʃis ol25
holie apoſtolicke ſea and the bi- Blandus
shop of Rõedo hold the primacie

T   3

of the vvhole vvorld , & that he
is the succeſſor of S. Peter prince
of the apoſtles, and the true vicar of Chriſt, and the head of the
vvhole church , the father & the
doctor of all chriſtiãs, vnto vvhõ
vvas giuen full povver by S.Peter
his auctoritie, to feed, direct, & go
uerne the vniuerſall church as it

Math-16.
18. Eph.
Ioh.20.

is cõtained in the actes of the holic councels, and ſacred cãnost. his
farre the ſaied councel. this is the
church that vvas founded by
Chriſt & builded vppon a firme
rocke & as he promiſed ſo vvee
ought to beleeue, that hell gates
shall neuer preuaile againſt it.
the certitude of vvhich trueth,
yve knovve by experiẽce & by the
vvoũderfull cõtinuãce, & ſucceſ-

fion therof thefe 1606. not vvith
ftanding all Pagans, Sarafins, Ɡoa-
thes, Vãdals, Longobards Turkes
Ievves & hererickes do labour to
deftroy it: this is the church not
vvithout gods vvounderfull mercie, & fpeciall prouidence to your
immortall glorie you obey. and
vvhen all thefe Norrhen natiõs
haue reuolted frõ the obedienee
therof vvhich like the generation
of vipers or the brood of Pãther,
do endeauour to kill and deftroy
their mother, thatdid ingẽder thẽ
of vvhome the prophet faieth *fi-
lios enutriui, &c.* I haue brought *Ifai.ʒ*
vp children yea and I haue e-
xalted thẽ to high vocations, but
they haue defpifed me, and being
compaffed vvith thefe rebellious

T 4

vn naturall children yet you profeſſe your catholicke faith & ac-
Knovvledge your mother in your
greateſt troubles and miſeries, of
vvhich you are a ſpectacle to all
natiõs. & as certaine riuers in the
midſt of great ſeas do retaine their
freſh vvaters, vvhich they haue
brought from the mother ſpring;
ſo you in the midſt of thieſe tē-
peſtuous vvaues of bitter hereſies
do obſerue & Keepe the milke of

Beda in vi-
ta S Patric
yourcatholick religiõ, vvhich you
haue ſuckt from your mother by
the preaching of S. Patrick, vvho
obtained of god by his feruēt pra
iers in vvhich he ſpent many ni-
ghtes, that the inhabirātes of Ire-

S Vincent
ſermo de
antechriſto
lād ſhould neuer forſak their faith,
& that the povver of antechriſt

should neuer cō thither, ſo as it is
an infallible conſequēce an Irish
man ergo a Papiſt, that any noble
man or gentleman to be a prote-
ſtāt or an heretick to be *rara auis* Rom.1
aſtrāge bird. vvherfore as S. Paule
gaue god thanckes for the faith of
the Romaines, and that the ſame
should be declared, & preached
in the vniuerſall vvorld, ſo I
ought to giue thanckes vnto god,
that this Romaine faith is not extinguished in poore Ireland, let
your neighbour cuntries aboūd in
vvealth, &pleaſures of this vvorld
& do you hold your faith in your
pouertie&calamitie:better it isto
be rich in faith, & poore as Lazarus, and to be in the boſome of
Abraham, then to be tormēted in

T 5

hell as the rich glutton vvas. Moy
fes did chufe to be poore in the
defarte, rather then to be rich in
Pharaos pallace, better be in prifon vvith Baptifta thē to be daun-
fing in the courte vvith cruell
Herod & his concubine, better it
is to vveepe vvith Chrieft, in the
gard en of Gethfemani, that vvas
put to death by the mightie
princes of this vvorld, then to be
aduánced vnto the office of a pro
moter vvithIudas: he that came to
be borne of a poore fimple virgin
that vvas deliuered in a crib his
purpofe vvas not to giue vs vaine
& corruptible riches, but rather
to diffuade vs frō them, vvhich he
defpifeth vvhē they be great im-
pedimentes, to our faluation. ther

fore hold, & embrace the riches
of your catholick faith for as S.
Aug.and S.Chryfoſt,do ſaye,ther
is no greater riches of thisvvorld,
nor no greater felicitie, then the
catholick religion.therfore the a-
apoſtle ſaieth *Deus replet vos omni*
gaudeo in credendo you haue a diuine & heuenlie conſolatiō by your
faith.hovv glad vvas the Eunuch
for receauing his fayth? it is the
treaſure thatvvas foūd ın the goſpell and for ioy therof,and to buy
it,the man that found ıt , ſold all
that he had. neyther can there be
greater plague,peſtilence,or miſe-
rie then heretickes,& the ſame to
be vvourſe then phariſees, publi-
ca is or any other ſinners vvhat
o euer:S. Aug. proues it lib. 2. de

Rom.1§
ato. 5.
Math.13

Chryſoſt
hom.1.50 ad
populum
Antioch.
Aug.ſer.de
veritsapoſt
& ſerm.de
tēp 181.c.12
ı n ancoram.
Vıct lib 3
de perʼectu
vandalica
Hıſt.Eccleſ.
lib. 7 c. 0
ın mar Ro
ma.12 ʼan
uarıi Smʼ
tom.1

ciuitate Dei cap c. 25. and Chryſ.
&ʔas Victor a voucheth Euagrius
& Surius do cōfirme. god tēpteth
you ſaieth Moyſes vnto the people of Iſraell by false prophetes
that it may be knovven vvhether
you loue him vvith all your heartes Deut. 13. and as the apoſtle
ſaith 1. Cor. 11. that heretickes
muſt be that ſuch as be good may
be tried.in this occaſiōshevv your
ſelues the ſeruantes of almightie
god, that should make more ac-
compt of his honour, and of the
profeſſion of your faith,thē of all
the vvorld , & the pleaſures therof,vvhich do paſſe a vvay in an
inſtāt,but the paine for the ſame
cōtineueth for euer vvhich is like
Moyſes his rodde,vvhē it vvas in

Exod 4 le-
uit 2 27

his handes it did feeme as a rodd,
but vvhen he did caft it from him
turned vnto a ferpent:fo that our
ioy in this life paffeth a vvay quic
klie as the fcripture doth fay *gaudiū*
hypocrytæ adinstar punEti the ioy
of a finner ended in an inftāt, but
his paine doth alvvaife continue:
let not the vaine hope of humane
fauour: or the dolefull blafte of
earthlie vanities, feparat youre fel
ues from Chrieft, or alienate you
frō his facred fpoufe the catholike
church: Knovving that by your
death ther muft be a deuorfe be-
tvvxit you, and all thevvorlde. but
novve rather, then ther should be
a feparation bet vvxit you & god
forfake all thinges vvhatfoeuer. &
as S. Em. faith *nec fi toto mundo renū-* ^{en vita D}
^{Ant}

tiantes possumus recompensare ali-
quid dignū cælestibus: if vve forsake
the vvhole vvorld, it is not a sufficient recōpence for the heuēlie
tabernacles. therefore offer your
selues vnto god preuenting thē
necessitie of your death as old A-
braham did offer Isaac vnto him,
vvhich vvas the deerest oblation
he had, & as Chriest did offer him

1. Pet. c. 3 self for vs, Chrieft by his blessed
oblation vvas glorified & you re-
deemed, & the father eternall sa-
tilsfied: & as S. Peter saieth Chrieft
suffreth for you, giuing vs an exā-
ple to follovv hī: let vs follovv his
blessed crosse. vvhich is our stādart
for by it vvee shall ouercome our
enimies, more strength therin, thē
in all the povver of the deuill: mo-

re force in the rodde of Moyses:
then in all thé armie of Pharao,
more valour in poore Iudith:thé
in all the povver ofHolophernes:
more kingdomes did your faith
subdue, then all the emperours of
the vvorld,more diuine auctoritie
yt hath,thé all the hereticxes that
euer vvere,more reason haue you
to profese it,thé they haue to impugne it : therfore feare nothing
for the Lyon of the tribe of Iuda
did ouercome : vvho trjumpheth
ouer the povver of antichrieft:
vvho ouercommeth allthe armie
of darknesse,and novve, is crovvned for the victorie he harh gotté
by his bleffed combate,vvhich be
holdeth your ftrife,& is readie to
giue euerie one that fighteth ma-

302 *A Mnemosynum* to the
fullie a blessed revvard vvhich
I humblie craue for
you and my self,
Amen.

F I N.

THE EPISTLE OF
Sainct Cyprian to the Thiba-
ritans vvritten vnto them
in the 2. persecution of Affri-
que, vvherin he exhorted
them to suffer martyrdome.

Haue often vvished *Epist 56.* (most louing Brethe- *li.4.Epist* ren)if time and leasu- *6.* re vvould so permit, to come vnto you, according to your desire, that I may streng- then, and confirme you vvith my presence. but because I am de- tained:as vvell, by vrgent occa- sions:as also,by the charge of the

V

flocke cōmitted vnto me by almi
ghtie god: I do send these letters
my attourney vnto you, and seing
our lord vouchsafed to stirre vs
vp, & also to admonishe me; that
I should be carefull of your conscience. Be it knovven vnto you,
and beleue certainelie, that the
dayes of affliction do hang, and
houer ouer your heades. the ruine of the vvorld & the time of an
tichrist approcheth, that euerie
one of vs, should prepare him self
for the battaile : and that vve
should meditate nothinge els, but
the glorie of eternal, life and the
crovvne of the confession of our
faith, neither should vve thincke,
the danger to come to be such
asvvēt before, for novve the fight

is more fierce, and harder, vnto
vvhich the souldiours of Chri-
ste, vvith a stedfast faith, and a
stoute courage ought to prepare
them selues, consideringe, that, as
they drincke the blood of Christ,
so they ought to shed their blood
for Christ and as S. Iohn saieth 1.*Ioh.*2.
vvhosoeuer vvill continue vvith
Christ ought to vvalke as he did
vvalke: the like the Apostle ex- *Rom.* 8.
horted, saieng, then are vve the
children, and heires of god, and
fellovvheires of Christ, vvhē trulie
vve suffer vvith Christ, that vve
may be glorified vvith Christ, all
vvhich ought novve at this time
to be considered of vs, that none
should desire any thing of this
vvorld, vvhich perisheth, but that

V 2

he should vvalke and follovve
Chrift, vvhich liueth for euer: &
alfo giueth life to his feruantes,
for the time is come (moft louing
bretheren) of vvhich Chrift long

10.16. fince forevvarned vs, fayeng, the
houre shall come, that all that
shall kill you, shall thincke he
doth great feruice to god: but
thefe thinges they shall do becaufe they knovve not my father
not me. let none therfore maruai-
le, that vve should be ouerpreffed
vvith perfecutions: turmoiled
vvith anguishes: afflicted vvith
greef: oppreffed vvith forrovves,
feeng that Chrift, by the authoritie of his vvordes, did foretell
thefe troubles to come, & fo did

i. Te 4. inftruct vs againft the battaile S.

Peter also his Apostle haue
taught, that there must be persecutions, that vve by our deathe
and suffering should be vnited
vnto the loue of god through the
example of the iust, that vvēt before, for he hath vvritten in his e-
pistles sayeng, most louing do not
meruaile, that euils do come vppō you, vvhich are for your triall,
neither be dismayed, as thoughe
they vvere strange & vnusuall, &
vvhensoeuer you are partakers of
Christ his passion, let it be vnto
you the greatest oecasion of ioy.
blessed are you, if you be reuiled
in the name of Christ. bécause
the name of his maiestie and vertue doth dvvell in you. vvhich
is blasphemed by them, is ho-

noured by vs. the Apostles haue
deliuered vnto vs those thinges,
vvhich they them selues did receaue from the mouth of our
lord saieng vvhosoeuer shall forsa
ke house or home, parētes, or brethren, vvife, or children for the
Kingdome of god shall receaue
in the vvorld to com life euerlasting. Blessed (saith he) you shall
be, vvhen men shall hate you, and
shall speake euill of you, and shall
banishe you for the sonne of
manhis sake.

Our lord vvoulde haue vs reioice and be glad in persecution.
for then the crovvnes of faith are
giuen, the soldiers of god are tried.
the heauens them selues stand o-
pen for Martirs.

Are not vve for this end pressed
to the christiã vvarfare, vve onght
not to expect a continuall peace,
but rather arme your selues for a
daylie skirmishe, seeng that our
sauiour him selfe hat he first giuē
the onsett: and being the master
of humilitie, patience, and longe
suffering, vvhat ought to be don
he put it in exceution.

Before he exhorted vs to take
vp his crosse, him selfe vvas crucified vppon the same. haue before
your eies most louing brethren
that he onelie, vvhich hath recea
ued all iudgments of his father, &
he vvhich is to come to iudge: &
vvhich hath al readie pronoūced
his iugement, and fore knovvledge: fortellinge, and making prote-

V 4

ſtation that he vvill confeſſe before his father, ſuche as confeſſe
him, and deny ſuche as vvill deny
him.

If vvee can eſchevve deathe,
then vve may lavvfully feare deathe. but ſeinge ſuche as are mortall muſt needes die: let vs ēbrace
ſuche à preſent occaſiō of à bleſſed death, that god his faithfull
promiſe may be accompliſhed:
& the revvard of immortalitie by
the end of our death performed.
Let vs not feare to die, vvhen by
our deathe vve ſhall be aduanced
vnto a crovvne, let neither any be
troubled, if happily he ſeeth the
people of Chriſt ſcattered, or the
holy aſſemblies of the church to
be broken vp, or the biſhops or

prieftes not teaching according to the cuftome, for if any
brother be feparated through ne-
ceffitie from the flocke of Chrift
in body, but not in fpirit: let him
not be difmayed nothing at all:&
thoughe he be alone in the vvil-
derneffe, let him not be afraid. he
is not alone, vvho hath Chrift for
his companion, and althogh in
his flight he shall fall to the hädes
of theues, brute beaftes should
fet vppon him, hunger, colde, &
thirft should afflict him, or the
rage of the fea shoulde ouervvhel
me him, let him be afsured
Chrift beholdeth the fouldier
vvherfoeuer he fighteth & doth
revvarde him vvhich dieth for
his name fake.

V 5

In persecutió it is no lesse glory
for martyrdome, to die alone, thē
to die publiklie amongest many,
for Christ is a sufficient vvitnesse
Gene.4. to a martyr, that doth acknovvledge and crovvne the martyr.

Let vs therfore louing bretthe-
Gene 22· ren imitate the iust Abel, vvhich
vvas the first martyr that suffred
for iustice. Let vs embrace the
example of the three children,
Ananias, Asarias, and Mysael,
vvhich neither being terrified by
there tender yeares, nor broken
by there captiuitie in the thral-
dome of Iurie, and the inhabitan-
tes of Hierusalem: vvith the vertue of a constant faithe refused to
adore the image, vvhich Nabu-
chodonosor the kinge caused to

be made, vvhoſe threatninge and
tormentes coulde not force them
to do againſt there conſcience,
faieng vve ought not ô Kinge to
diſpleaſe god vvhome vve ſerue
to pleaſe man, for our god vvhome vve adore, is able to deliuer vs
from the furie of this fire : and if
not, be it Knovven vnto you, vve
vvill not obey your vnlavvfull
commande, they did beleue that
accordinge to their faithe, they
coulde be deliuered, and if not
that the kinge shoulde knovve
that they vvere ready to die for
his honour vvhome they vvor-
shipped, for in this conſiſteth the
ſtrength and vertue of faithe, to
beleue that god can deliuer vs
from this preſent deathe, and yet

not to feare the fame, nor to be ouercome by it, that the force of faith may be knovven. Daniel alfo, vvhen beinge ftreightlie commanded to vvorfhip the Idoll in the defence of gods honour, & vvith full liberty of faith burfte out fayeng: I honour nothing but my lorde god, vvhich made heauen & earth. vvhat should I fpeake of the moft bleffed martyrs mentioned in the Machabees: & the manifold paines, and tormentes of the feauen bretheren, and their mother comforting, & ftrē gthning them, in the middeft of there outragious tormētes, & her felfe likevvife dieng vvith her children. Do not thefe great examples of vertue and ʃfaith

vvitnesse and exhort vs to the
triumphe of martyrdome, vvhat
shal I say of the proph ets, vvhich
the holy spirit did inspire to foretell thinges to com, as alsothe apo
stles vvhich godhath chosé. do not
the iust vvhich are killed for iustice teachevs also to die? Christ had
his beginingesfrō the martyrdome
of the infantes, that frō too yeares dovvnvvard & vnder, vvere all
put to the svvorde, vvhose age beinge vnfitt for the battaile, vvas
foūde fitt and made vvorthy of a
crovvne, that it may be knovvē,
that they vvere innocentes that
vvere Killed forChrist, by vvhich
it is manifest that none is exempted from the danger of persecution, vvhē suche doe suffre mar-

tyrdome:vvhat a greeuous thinge
it is for a christian that the seruāt
vvill not follovve the maister, &
disdaineth to do,that vvhich his
maſter hath don, & that vvevvill
not ſuffer for our ſinnes vvhich
vvas the cauſe of Chriſt his ſuffe-
ringe.the ſonne of god,did ſuffer
to make vs the ſonnes of god,and
the ſonne of man vvill not ſuffer,
that he may continue the ſonne
of god,if ſo vve be troubled that
the vvorld hateth vs , it hated
Chriſt before,if vve ſuſtayne reproches, tormentes, banishmen-
tes:more greuous thē theſeChriſt
did ſuffer beinge the lorde and
maker of thevvorlde,if thevvorld
hate you(ſaith he,)Knovve you it
hated me fiſt , if you had bene

of the vvorld,the vvorlde vvould
loue that vvhich is his ovvne:but
becaufe you are not of the vvorld
and I haue chofen you out of the
vvorlde,and therfore the vvorlde
hateth you.remēber the fpeeches
I had vvith you,the feruant is not
greater then the maifter , if they
haue perfecuted me : they shall
alfo perfecute you,vvhat foeuer
our lord hath done , or taught,
ought not to excufe the difciple,
if he shoulde omitt the fame. I
meane fuche,as do learne and do
not accordinglie. Let none
moft louing bretheren be terrified for feare of future perfecutiō
or the cōming of antichrift,& let
euery one be armed , both by e-
uangelicall exhortatiōs,& diuine

preceptes, against all occasions:
antechrist commeth: but Christ
shall ouercome. Let the enimie
exercise his mallice vppon vs: our
lord doth follovve to reuenge
our deathe & sufferinge. our ad
uersary threateneth in his furie,
but there is one that can deliuer
vs from his handes. he is rather to
be feared, vvhose anger none can
eschevve, him selfe vvillinge vs
not to feare those, that killed the
body, but they can not Kill the
soule. but ratherto fearehim, that
can destroy both soule & body
in hell. & againe vvhosoeuer loueth his ovvne life, shall loose it
& vvho soeuer hateth his life in
this vvorlde, shall preserue the same for life euerlastinge.

Vvhen

Vvhen men do exerciſe them ſelues for a ſecular combat, they thincke it a great honour & glory if in the vievv of the emperour, and preſence of the people he be crovvned.

Behold an honorablè vvourthy combat, the revvard vvherof is no leſſe vvorth then an euer laſtinge crovvne : god beholdeth vs fighting , and caſting his eie vppon ſuche, that he vouchafeth to make his ovvn childrē, doth enioy the ſpectacle of our ſtrife.

In this chalenge of our faith vve be made a ſpectacle vnto god, vnto Chriſt, and his holy angels. hovv great an honour is it to enter into the battell in the preſence of god, and to be crovvned by

X

Chrift the iudge of our chalengè,
let vs arme our felues moft louing bretheren vvithall force and
ftrength, and let vs prepare our
felues for the fight , vvith an in-
corrupt minde ,fincere faith, and
deuout affection.as the armie of
god marched in the vantgard, let
thofe that did euer ftand arme
them felues,leaft they should fall
Let thofe that are fallen,prepare
them felues that they may reco-
uer vvhat they haue loft , let the
honour of the victorie gotten,
prouoke the onevnto the battay-
le,& griefe of the battrell loft fol-
licite thother vnto the combat.
the Apoftle admonisheth vs:
faieng our vvarre is not againft
fleash , and bloud, but againft

povvers, and princes of darknesof
this vvorlde againſt the vvicked
ſpirits, that are in the ayre, for
vvhich cauſe put on gods armou
re, that you may be able to reſiſt
in the euill day : that hauing ended your troubles, you may ſtād
vvith your loynes girded in
truth , and hauing put on the
helmet of iuſtice : and being
ſhod in the preparation of the
goſpel of peace, taking vnto your
ſelues, the ſhielde of faith, vvherein you may extinguish al the
fierie dartes of the vvicked, arme
your ſelues vvith the ſallet of
ſaluation, and the ſvvorde of the
ſpirit, vvhich is the vvord of god
theſe be the vveapons vvee
ſhould take in hand.

Let vs defend our felues by
is the fpirituall and heauenly ar-
mour. Let vs put onthe helmet of
iuftice, that our heart may be defended and guarded againft the
fpeare of the enemie. Let our feet
be shod and armed by the euangelicall authoritie, that vvhen vve
shall begin, to tread vnder foote
the ferpent, she shall not be able
to bite, nor to ftinge vs, let v s bea
re manfully the shield of faith,
being couered vvithall, thatvvhat
foeuerdarte the enemye shall caft
may be extinguished : Let vs receaue the helmet of faluation for
the defence of our head, that our
eares may not heere the cruell
edictes. let vs make a couenant
vvith our eyes, that they may not

fee deteftablie fimblances, let vs
arme our fore head , vvith the fi-
gne of the croffe , let our mouth
beKept,that our inuincible tonge
may confeffe our lord Chrift Ie-
fu.Let vs fortifye our right hand
vvith the fpirituall fvvord that it
may reiect all abominable facrifices. and being mindfull of the
eucharift , that fuche as receaue
our lordes body,they may after·
vvard receaue our lordes revvard
of an euerlaftinge crovvne.ô day
hovv happy thou shalt be vvhen
our lord shall begin to reckon his
people,and by due examination
of his diuine Knovvledge to ac-
Knovvledge euery our defertes,
to caft the guiltie perfons vnto
the flames of euerlafting fire , &

X 3

our perfecutours vnto endles pay
nes:and to fatisfy and pay vntovs,
the revvard of our faith and deuotion. vvhat great ioy vvill you
feele,to be admitted tofee god,to
be honoured vvith the ioy of faluation,and eternall light, vvith
Chrift our lorde?to falute Abraham,Ifaac,and Iacob, and all the
patriarches,and prophets,and A-
poftles,and martyrs;and to reioice vvith the iuft and friendes of
god in the celeftiall Throne, to
enioy the pleafure ofthe imorta-
litye promifed, and the eternity
defired,to poffeffe thatvvhich the
eie can not fee, neither the eare
cã heare,neither the heart of mã
can conceaue,for the tribulatiõs
of this time(as theApoftlefaieth)

are not anſvverable vnto the glory vvhich shalbe receaued, vvhen
the brightnes shall shine vppō vs,
then vve shalbe bleſſed, and ioyfull, that god hath vouchafed
to honoure vs, as like vvife the
vvicked, that haue forſaken god
vnto vvhome they are rebells, &
perſourminge the vvill of the deuill, shalbe tormented by an vn-
quenchable fire vvith him: haue
theſe alvvayes in your heartes. Let
this be your continuall medita-
tion to haue allvvayes before
your eies, the punishmentes of
the vvicked, and of ſuche as deny
Chriſt, vvhat glory is promiſed
vnto thoſe, that confeſſe their faith. if in meditatiōof theſe thīges
the time of perſecutiō shall come

X 4

the souldier of Christ being suffi-
ciently instructed, vvith his prece
ptes, and admonitions shall not
tremble at the fight, but shalbe
prepared for the crovvne;
farevvell most louing
bretheren.

FIN.